Floribbean Flavors

A reflection of Florida's new cuisine
Tony Merola

First Edition
First Printing: 1996
10,000 Copies

Copyright ©1996
Brooks Tropicals/Tony Merola
P.O. Box 18400
Homestead, Florida 33090-0160

Library of Congress Number: 96-086522
ISBN: 0-9654211-0-4

Photography by Lanny Provo and Mark Huselbeck

Manufactured and designed in the United States of America by
FRP™
2451 Atrium Way
Nashville, Tennessee 37214
1-800-798-1780

Cover Design and Art Direction: Steve Newman
Book Design: Starletta Polster
Project Manager: Ashlee Brown
Production Design: Bill Kersey

Additional copies of Floribbean Flavors may be obtained from
Brooks Tropicals, Inc. 1-800-327-4833

Contents

The Seasons of Floribbean

As the weather warms and the earth begins to burst with color, make your meals lively and fresh with tropical fruits.

Hot weather is what South Florida is all about! Eat light and refreshing Floribbean meals and stay cool like native Floridians.

Tropical fruits and vegetables are plentiful right through fall. Cooking with tropicals is as colorful as a forest in autumn.

Warm up winter with hearty vegetables and succulent fruits. Enjoy a taste of the tropics!

Dedication

I dedicate this book to Pal Brooks,

a true modern day pioneer

whose innovative growing practices

have made these

delightful products available today.

Preface

Few would guess that the country's largest native tropical fruit and vegetable grower, Brooks Tropicals, had humble beginnings. Even fewer would guess that its president, Pal Brooks, would build a tiny tin shed into a sprawling facility producing millions of dollars in tropical fruit and vegetable sales. Yet, that is precisely what Pal did. The story of Pal and his father, J. R. Brooks, encompasses the American dream.

During Thanksgiving week of 1928, a young man with only a single employee and a broad vision started a fruit-packing business. Undaunted by the steamy weather and endless supply of mosquitoes, J. R. Brooks made history in the heart of Homestead, Florida, by shipping one hundred boxes of fresh Florida avocados via rail to New York, at a time when such produce items were novelties.

The response was overwhelming, and J. R. soon increased his staff and land holdings to accommodate the demand. Just as J. R.'s future seemed bright, the Great Depression settled in over Dade County. However, J. R. Brooks was not easily discouraged, and remained committed to his vision and to his business. The J. R. Brooks Company survived the Depression, and continued to grow an abundance of limes and avocados for the American public.

The year 1945 was one of devastation. The company was brought to its knees by a powerful hurricane, which was subsequently characterized as the biggest catastrophe in South Florida's history. It was the first of a series of natural disasters that the Brooks family would have to face.

After graduating from the University of Florida in 1961, J. R.'s son Pal began work with the company. Pal didn't begin his career sitting behind a fancy desk in a big office, but rather learned every aspect of the tropical fruit business by working in the fruit groves and the packing house. In 1967, Pal was passed the family baton when he purchased the company.

Pal's vision for the company expanded upon that of his father. Pal saw a market for the many different tropical fruits and vegetables that flourished in his backyard and in those of his fellow Floridians. His vision was to take these backyard fruits, and introduce them to the rest of America. Commercialization could only be accomplished through marketing, education and improved technology.

The company spearheaded research and development efforts, as well as the marketing of tropicals, at a time when such endeavors did not exist. Pal's in-depth knowledge catapulted the tropical fruit industry in South Florida to new heights. Brooks Tropicals' early research and marketing efforts centered around star fruit in the 1980s. Its wide acceptance stunned the industry. Today, Brooks Tropicals has added to that success story with mangoes, papayas, passion fruit, guava and many others.

In 1988, fire nearly destroyed Pal's dreams. Again, he used disaster as an opportunity to rebuild a state-of-the-art facility to accommodate the unique handling procedures required by tropical fruits and vegetables. His facility served as a model for other tropical packing houses until the devastating winds of Hurricane Andrew blew in August 1992. Hurricane Andrew pounded Brooks Tropicals with wind gusts clocked at two hundred miles per hour, leaving the company with millions of dollars in damages in less than six hours.

Accustomed to turning tragedy into triumph, Pal surveyed the situation, and looked for solutions. Left with most of his trees destroyed, Pal was forced to look elsewhere for product, and decided to increase his tropical fruit and vegetable imports. Necessity grew into opportunity as he was able to bring into the United States a wider variety of fruits and vegetables. His business allowed him to import the best of what other countries had to offer. Pal's foresight has always been invaluable to his company. Today, Brooks Tropicals' groves are once again flourishing, and tropical fruits and vegetables from Homestead and from Central and South America are shipped daily to supermarkets across the United States.

Acknowledgments

Countless individuals have made the tropical fruit and vegetable industry a reality in South Florida. Their vision, hard work and ability to persevere against the wiles of nature have helped to make possible a book about the new Florida cuisine. I would like to recognize a few special people that support our company and continue to contribute to Brooks Tropicals' success.

Bill Krome, one of the original pioneers of South Florida's community of tropical fruit growers, spearheaded the development of both the Florida avocado and mango industries since the mid-1930s. Bill is still a leading grower today. Franco Biocchi, a great friend of the company, has provided our company with beautiful limes and avocados since the mid-1970s. To the delight of all, Marc and Kiki Ellenby of LNB Groves, continue to grow rare and uncommon tropical fruits. Alcides Acosta, a lime grower and friend, continually provides Brooks Tropicals with quality fruit, as well as with insight.

Special thanks to my photographers, Lanny Provo and Mark Huselbeck. Lanny's exquisite styling and photographic flare, along with his attention to detail, are evident throughout this book. Mark Huselbeck's beautiful photography of the food richly enhances the book's aesthetic appeal. Much appreciation to Richard and Susan Rogers of Rogers Graphics of Vashon Island, Washington. Their creativity and insightful guidance continue to promote our company image. Thanks to Carole Kotkin for editing and fine-tuning my recipes, and to Cindy Ritter for helping me plan my menus.

A very special thank you to Craig Wheeling, C.E.O. of Brooks Tropicals, whose commitment and support made this book a reality. Thanks to all the employees at Brooks Tropicals that gave limitless hours to bring this book together: Robin Sprague for making my words and thoughts say Floribbean, and for paying attention to details and deadlines; Don Evans for his business savvy, hard work and enthusiasm on this project; and Alyson Albregts, who diligently persevered through endless rewrites.

Much love and gratitude go to the most influential women in my life: my wife Mary Lou, for her words of support and ability to withstand long hours in the kitchen with me, and for her knack for knowing exactly what I need in the kitchen and in my life; my daughter Jennifer, for being the apple of my eye; and my mother Filomena, for her love of cooking.

And finally, special recognition and thanks to Gerald Gliber, who served as my mentor and inspiration while I was a student at the New York Restaurant School.

Introduction

South Florida sizzles with a diverse combination
of people from countries throughout Central and South
America, the Caribbean, Cuba, and of course the
United States! "Floribbean" is a new cuisine that reflects the
favorite foods and unique cooking styles that
have naturally emerged from the area's rich cultural blend.

Fresh tropical produce has always been the key ingredient in
various Latino cooking styles, and remains an integral
part of Floribbean. Today, Floribbean cooking is found as far
north as New York City, and as far west as Los Angeles.

The following recipes provide a tasty glimpse into South
Florida life. You will be introduced to the world of Floribbean,
as well as to how South Floridians like to eat. Every plate
will be colorful, ethnic, and bursting with new flavors. Floribbean's
brilliant colors and tempting flavors beckon you to visit
our tropical shores, if just for 30 minutes in your own kitchen.

Floribbean Spring

As the weather warms
and the earth begins to burst
with color, make your
meals lively and fresh with
tropical fruits.

Springtime Dinner

Mango Cheesecake adds
a glorious finale to
this springtime dinner menu.

Spring Greens Salad*

Ginger, Lime and Uniq Fruit-Scented
Rack of Lamb

or

Sautéed Red Snapper with Cilantro Butter Sauce

Saffron Risotto*

Steamed Asparagus*

Mango Cheesecake

*indicates menu suggestions for which there are no recipes

Ginger-Lime and Uniq Fruit-Scented Rack of Lamb

The rack, or rib roast is a very tender and elegant cut. Ask the butcher to remove the chine bone from each rack, to trim and "French" the ribs, remove the fell, and trim the fat to no more than ¼ inch in thickness. To present the racks standing upright, slice a thin wedge of meat off the bottom of the eye. This creates a flat base and simplifies carving.

1 (1-inch) stalk fresh ginger
2 medium cloves garlic
1 large Uniq fruit
1 large lime
2 tablespoons soy sauce
1 tablespoon dark sesame oil
2 racks of lamb (about 1¼ pounds each), chine bones removed and ribs "Frenched"

Preparation: Peel the ginger and garlic. Remove three 1x2-inch strips of zest from the lime. Squeeze ⅓ cup Uniq juice into the workbowl of a food processor fitted with the metal blade. Add the ginger, garlic, soy sauce, and sesame oil, and process until smooth. Put the lamb in a large bowl and rub the meat with the ginger paste. Refrigerate, covered, for 24 hours, turning the racks of lamb occasionally in the seasoning paste.

Cooking: Bring meat to room temperature. Adjust oven rack to high position and heat oven to 450 degrees. Wrap the rib bones in foil to prevent blackening and put the racks of lamb meat side up in a shallow roasting pan. Spread any remaining ginger paste over the meat and roast for 10 minutes. Lower oven to 350 degrees and roast until the internal temperature of the meat at the thickest point registers 130 degrees (medium-rare), 15 to 20 minutes.

Serving: Let racks rest 5 minutes, cut into chops and serve immediately.

Yield: 4 servings.

Sautéed Red Snapper with Cilantro Butter Sauce

Sauce
1¹/₂ cups dry white wine
¹/₂ cup chopped fresh cilantro
1 tablespoon whipping cream
1 tablespoon chopped shallots
¹/₂ bay leaf

Fish
3 tablespoons olive oil
4 (6-ounce) opakapaka or red snapper fillets
¹/₂ cup (1 stick) chilled unsalted butter, cut into pieces

For sauce: Boil all ingredients in heavy medium saucepan until liquid is reduced to 3 tablespoons, about 10 minutes. Strain through sieve set over heavy small saucepan, pressing on solids with back of spoon. May be prepared 1 day ahead. Cover and refrigerate.

For fish: Heat oil in heavy large skillet over medium-high heat. Season fish with salt and pepper. Add fish to skillet and cook until cooked through, about 4 minutes per side.

Meanwhile, bring sauce to simmer. Gradually add butter 1 piece at a time, whisking just until melted.

Spoon sauce onto plates. Place fish atop sauce.

Yield: 4 servings.

Mango Cheesecake

Brooks mango purée adds a delicious tropical flavor to this luscious creamy cheesecake. To prevent cracking across the center of the cheesecake, don't open the oven door while the cheesecake is in the oven. When it is removed from the oven, run a knife along the edge of pan so that the cake can pull away freely as it shrinks.

1 tablespoon unsalted butter or cooking spray
2 pounds cream cheese at room temperature
1/2 cup sugar
1/4 pound unsalted butter, softened
4 eggs
1 teaspoon vanilla
Juice from 1/2 Brooks lime
3 tablespoons flour
3 tablespoons cornstarch
1 pound sour cream
8 tablespoons Brooks mango purée

Adjust middle rack of oven to middle position and heat oven to 325 degrees. Grease a 9-inch springform pan with butter or coat with cooking spray. Insert metal knife blade in food processor bowl. Process cream cheese 30 seconds. Scrape down sides of container. With machine running, add sugar and butter and process 10 seconds longer. Scrape down sides of container. With processor running, add eggs, vanilla, lime juice, flour and cornstarch. Process 15 seconds. Scrape down sides of container. Process 5 seconds longer. Add sour cream and mango purée and pulse until incorporated.

Pour mixture into prepared pan and bake for 1 hour. Turn oven off and leave cheesecake in oven, with door closed, for 1 hour. DO NOT OPEN OVEN DOOR. Remove from oven and cool completely in pan. Cover and refrigerate for 12 hours or up to 2 days. Remove side of pan and place cake on serving platter.

Yield: 10 servings.

Mango Purée

Cut the mango on both sides of the pit. Reserve a few slices for decoration. Scoop out all the rest of the flesh and purée in a blender or food processor fitted with the metal knife blade.

Patio Luncheon

Velvety Mango Mousse
adds the perfect finishing touch to
a refreshing spring lunch.

Papaya-Pork Salad with
Green Peppercorn Dressing

Sesame Rolls*

Mango Mousse

Chocolate-Dipped Biscotti*

Cappuccinos*

*indicates menu suggestions for which there are no recipes

Papaya-Pork Salad with Green Peppercorn Dressing

2 pounds boneless pork loin, fat trimmed
$1/3$ cup minced scallions
1 teaspoon minced fresh ginger
2 cloves garlic, minced
$1/4$ cup dry sweet vermouth
$1/4$ cup fresh lime juice
1 tablespoon grainy mustard
1 head radicchio
1 bunch watercress, large stems removed
2 papayas, peeled and seeded
1 teaspoon olive oil
Green Peppercorn Dressing

Cut pork into julienne slices, 1x$1/2$ inch. Combine scallions, ginger, garlic, vermouth, lime juice, and mustard in mixing bowl. Add pork and stir to coat with marinade. Let stand at least 30 minutes. Line platter with largest radicchio leaves. Tear remaining radicchio and the watercress into bite-sized pieces. Combine in mixing bowl. Peel and seed papayas. Cut 1 papaya into large dices; thinly slice other papaya and reserve for garnish. Add diced papaya to watercress mixture. Make Green Peppercorn Dressing (recipe follows). Drain pork. Heat oil in large skillet over medium-high heat. Add pork and stir-fry just until cooked through, about 5 to 6 minutes. Toss watercress mixture with half the salad dressing and place on radicchio on platter. Spoon pork over salad; garnish with papaya slices and pork. Serve immediately.

Yield: 4 servings.

Green Peppercorn Dressing

$1/2$ cup sour cream
2 teaspoons fresh lime juice
1 tablespoon green peppercorns, drained
1 teaspoon minced fresh ginger
1 teaspoon grainy mustard
$1/2$ teaspoon grated lime zest

Mix all ingredients in small bowl.

Mango Mousse

This rich and delicious tropical combination of flavors makes the perfect summer dessert. For a glamorous presentation, fill balloon wine glasses with the mousse and garnish with mango slices.

2 Brooks mangoes
2¹/₂ tablespoons honey
2 tablespoons fresh lime juice
1¹/₄ cups heavy cream
2 egg whites

Cut the mangoes on both sides of the pit. Reserve a few slices for decoration. Scoop out all the rest of the flesh and purée in a blender or food processor fitted with the steel blade. Add the honey and lime juice and purée until smooth. Whip cream to soft peaks; fold into mango mixture.

Beat egg whites until stiff. Stir half of whites into mousse, blending well. Fold in remaining egg whites, making sure there are no lumps. Spoon into individual dessert glasses or a serving bowl. Garnish with mango slices.

Yield: 8 servings.

Brunch at the Grove

Dazzle brunch-time guests with a taste of the tropics.

Champagne or Mimosas*

Uniq Fruit-Radicchio Salad

Chayote Frittata

Strawberry Tarts*

*indicates menu suggestions for which there are no recipes

Chayote Frittata

This tropical twist on an Italian favorite makes a great brunch or luncheon dish.

3 tablespoons olive oil
1 Brooks chayote, cut into strips
1 small sweet onion, chopped
1-inch piece of Brooks fresh ginger root, finely grated
1/2 red bell pepper, cut into strips
1/2 green bell pepper, cut into strips
6 large eggs
1/2 cup freshly grated Parmesan cheese
1/2 cup heavy cream
1/2 teaspoon salt
1/4 teaspoon freshly ground pepper
1 tablespoon olive oil

Heat 3 tablespoons olive oil in 10-inch flameproof heavy skillet (preferably nonstick) over medium heat. Add chayote, onion, ginger root and peppers, and sauté until vegetables are tender, about 5 minutes.

In a medium-sized bowl, beat eggs, cheese, heavy cream, and salt and pepper together. Remove vegetables with a slotted spoon and stir them into the egg mixture. Heat the remaining tablespoon of olive oil in the same skillet.

Pour in the egg mixture and cook, over medium-high heat, stirring lightly, just until the bottom is set and lightly browned, 6 to 8 minutes. The top should still be wet. Place the skillet under the broiler and cook until the frittata is golden and sizzling, about 2 minutes.

Reverse frittata onto serving plate. Cut into wedges and serve hot.

Yield: 6 to 8 servings.

Uniq Fruit-Radicchio Salad

Uniq fruit combines beautifully with grilled or sautéed onions and radicchio to make a delicious salad.

1 head radicchio lettuce (round kind)
2 Uniq fruits, peeled and sectioned
1 sweet onion, sliced into rings
¼ cup balsamic vinegar
2 tablespoons fresh lime juice
½ cup lite olive oil
Salt and pepper to taste

Cut the radicchio in half, carefully remove the outer leafs to form 4 nests (concave shape).

Arrange half of a Uniq fruit in the middle of each radicchio nest.

Grill or sauté sweet onions; divide into nests.

In a salad shaker, mix balsamic vinaigrette. Sprinkle the nests with the vinaigrette.

Yield: 4 servings.

Costa Rican Pasta

Fresh chayote squash gives a
flavorful new spin to traditional pasta.

Watercress and Beet Salad*

Chayote and Bowtie Pasta

Caribbean Shrimp

Crusty Sourdough Bread*

Fresh Fruit Compote*

*indicates menu suggestions for which there are no recipes

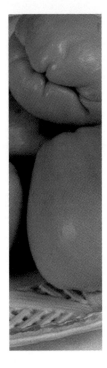

Chayote and Bowtie Pasta

This is a very simple pasta dish to make when you are short on time. The bow tie pasta catches and holds the sauce, bringing all the tastes together.

1/3 cup olive oil
1 large sweet onion, quartered and cut crosswise into thin slices
2 cloves garlic, finely chopped
1 red bell pepper, cut into thin strips
2 fresh Brooks chayote squash, peeled and cut into thin strips
1 small head of broccoli, cut into florets
1 tablespoon salt
1 pound bow tie pasta (farfalle)
1 1/2 ounces pignoli nuts (pine nuts)
1/4 pound prosciutto ham, cut into thin strips
Salt and freshly ground pepper to taste
1/3 cup freshly grated Parmesan cheese

Heat 1/2 tablespoon olive oil in a large skillet over medium heat; add the onion, garlic, pepper, chayote and broccoli. Sauté until the vegetables are tender, about 10 minutes; set aside.

Meanwhile, bring 4 quarts of water and 1 tablespoon salt to a boil. Add the pasta and cook according to package instructions until it is al dente (firm to the bite), about 12 minutes. Drain. In a large bowl, toss the cooked vegetables and pasta together. Add pignoli nuts, prosciutto, remaining olive oil and salt and pepper to taste. Mix well. Sprinkle with Parmesan cheese and toss again. Serve at once with additional cheese on the side.

Yield: 6 servings.

Caribbean Shrimp

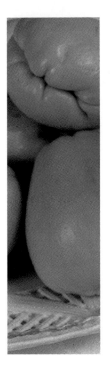

2 pounds fresh or frozen shrimp in shells
¼ cup salad oil
3 tablespoons white wine vinegar
2 tablespoons lime juice
1 scotch bonnet pepper, seeded and finely chopped
1 tablespoon honey
2 teaspoons Jamaican Jerk Seasoning
1 medium mango, peeled, pitted, sliced, and halved crosswise
1 small lime, halved lengthwise and sliced
1 small red onion, quartered and thinly sliced

In large saucepan cook fresh or frozen shrimp, uncovered, in lightly salted boiling water for 1 to 3 minutes or till shrimp turn pink. Drain immediately and cool. Peel shrimp, leaving tails intact; devein. Place shrimp in a heavy plastic bag. At this point, you can seal the bag and chill for up to 24 hours.

For marinade, in a screw-top jar combine salad oil, white wine vinegar, lime juice, scotch bonnet pepper, honey, and the Jamaican Jerk Seasoning. Cover and shake well to mix; pour over shrimp in plastic bag. Cover and chill for 1 hour, turning bag occasionally.

To serve, drain shrimp, reserving marinade. In a large serving bowl, layer shrimp, mango, lime slices, and onion, repeating until all are used. Drizzle reserved marinade on top.

Yield: 10 to 12 appetizer servings.

Jamaican Jerk Seasoning

Combine 2 teaspoons onion powder, 1 teaspoon sugar, 1 teaspoon ground thyme, 1 teaspoon salt, ½ teaspoon ground allspice, ¼ teaspoon ground cinnamon, and ¼ teaspoon ground red pepper.

Vegetarian Fare from the Grill

Fresh tropical ingredients elevate
vegetarian cuisine to new heights.

Chayote Burgers

Grilled Sweet Onions

Taro Shoestrings page 91

Coconut Macaroons*

Limeade page 58

*indicates menu suggestions for which there are no recipes

Chayote Burgers

Brooks chayote squash and Brooks fresh ginger root enhance the texture and flavor of this satisfying main course. It also makes an excellent filling for stuffed peppers, cabbages and other vegetables.

1 tablespoon olive oil
1 medium onion, chopped
1/2 pound portobello mushrooms, coarsely chopped
1/2 tablespoon Brooks fresh ginger root, finely chopped
1 cup corn kernels, either fresh or canned (drained)
1 cup Brooks chayote squash, peeled and cubed
1/2 cup chopped almonds, toasted
1 cup brown rice, cooked
1/4 cup black beans, cooked
1 1/2 cups cornflake crumbs
2 large eggs, beaten
Salt and freshly ground pepper to taste

Heat olive oil in a large sauté pan. Add the onion, stir to coat it with oil and sauté over medium heat until softened, 4 to 5 minutes. Add mushrooms and cook over high heat until they have browned and released their juices. Reduce heat to medium, add ginger root, corn, and Brooks chayote and sauté for about 4 minutes.

Insert metal knife blade in food processor bowl and add vegetable mixture and remaining ingredients. Pulse until the mixture looks like chopped meat. Form into patties. Place on grill or under broiler until nicely browned. Serve with grilled onions and tomatoes.

Yield: 8 to 10 burgers.

Grilled Sweet Onions

Chayotes are a staple vegetable in Central and South America, as well as the Caribbean Islands. Chayote can be used for dishes that would call for zucchini, but chayote is much firmer, and requires longer cooking time. It also stays firm and slightly crunchy, even if held for a short time before serving.

2 fresh Brooks chayotes
1 sweet onion (Walla Walla, Vidalia, or other sweet variety)
3 tablespoons olive oil
1 clove garlic, peeled and minced (about 1½ teaspoons)
¼ cup fresh basil, chopped
2 tablespoons fresh oregano, chopped
Salt and pepper to taste

Remove stems from chayotes, and slice into strips that are comfortably bite-size. Set aside. Peel onion and slice crosswise into narrow rounds. Cut rounds in half, making strips. Set aside.

Heat olive oil in a large deep skillet or wok. Add garlic and onion and sauté for 2 minutes. Add chayotes and continue cooking until vegetables are crisp tender. Add basil and oregano and sauté for 2 to 3 minutes. Add salt and pepper to taste. Serve immediately.

Yield: 8 servings.

Uniq Flavors

Top off a springtime
luncheon with a Florida favorite—
classic Key Lime Pie.

Yellow Pepper Soup

Avocado Halves filled with Shrimp Salad*

or

Fish with Ginger Beurre Blanc

Miniature Poppy Seed Rolls*

Key Lime Pie

Hot Tea*

or

Cucumber Limeade with Ginger

*indicates menu suggestions for which there are no recipes

Yellow Pepper Soup

4 yellow peppers, roasted, stemmed, seeded and peeled
1 cup granulated sugar
1/8 teaspoon powdered saffron
1 papaya, peeled and seeded
1 to 2 teaspoons lime zest
1 to 2 teaspoons orange zest
2 tablespoons fresh lime juice
4 tablespoons fresh orange juice
2 teaspoons Pernod
1/2 papaya, peeled, seeded and diced
1/4 cup plain yogurt

Simmer peppers, sugar and saffron in 2 cups water in nonreactive saucepan over medium heat for 10 minutes. Transfer water and peppers to a blender. Add whole papaya, lime and orange zests, lime and orange juices and Pernod; purée until smooth. Strain through strainer into nonreactive container; cool; refrigerate overnight. *To serve:* Ladle soup into chilled bowls; garnish with diced papaya and a swirl of yogurt. *Scale-up:* Scale up in direct proportion.

Yield: 4 servings.

Ginger Beurre Blanc

A ginger, vinegar and cream sauce for fish

1/4 cup minced fresh ginger
3 tablespoons white wine vinegar
1/4 cup heavy cream
1/4 pound butter
Salt and freshly ground black pepper to taste

Combine the ginger, vinegar and 2 tablespoons of water in a saucepan. Bring to a boil and cook over high heat until liquid has almost evaporated, about 2 minutes. Add the heavy cream and continue cooking over high heat until mixture is reduced by half, about 1 minute. Over the lowest heat possible whisk butter into the reduction, about a tablespoon at a time, adding another piece as each is almost incorporated. Butter should not melt completely but should soften to form a creamy sauce. Remove from heat and season to taste with salt and pepper. Strain sauce into a bowl and cover to keep warm.

Yield: 4 servings.

Key Lime Pie

We've developed our own healthy version of a Florida favorite using real key limes.

1 (14-ounce) can sweetened condensed milk
2 ounces Egg Beaters™
³/₄ cup Brooks key lime juice (approximately 12 to 15 key limes)
1 (9-inch) baked pie shell or graham cracker pie crust

To a mixing bowl, add condensed milk and Egg Beaters™. Add key lime juice to the bowl and mix just to blend. Do not over beat.

Pour mixture into 9-inch baked pie shell or graham cracker pie crust. Chill until set—overnight is best. Top with whipped cream if you like.

Yield: 8 servings.

Cucumber Limeade with Ginger

1 medium cucumber, peeled, seeded, and coarsely chopped
¹/₂ cup fresh lime juice
¹/₄ cup superfine sugar, or to taste
Juice squeezed from 2 teaspoons finely grated peeled fresh ginger root
10 ice cubes plus additional for serving

In a blender, purée cucumber with other ingredients (including the 10 ice cubes). Divide limeade between 2 glasses filled with additional ice cubes.

Yield: 2 servings.

Floribbean Summer

Hot weather is what
South Florida is all about!
Eat light and refreshing
Floribbean meals and stay cool
like native Floridians.

Seafood on the Grill

Grilled fish take on a whole
new attitude with a spirited mango
and hot pepper sauce.

Floribbean Grilled Eggplant Salad

Grilled Red Snapper with Hot Mango Sauce

Chilled Macaroni Vinaigrette Salad*

Lime Sherbet*

*indicates menu suggestions for which there are no recipes

Grilled Red Snapper

To prevent the fish from sticking to the grill and falling apart, be sure to oil the grill rack and turn the fish only once.

4 fillets of red snapper (about 2 pounds)
Salt and freshly ground pepper to taste
$^1/_3$ cup olive oil
$^1/_4$ cup fresh Brooks lime juice
$^1/_2$ tablespoon Brooks fresh ginger root, finely chopped
Hot Mango Sauce

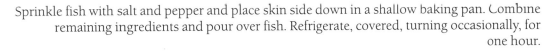

Sprinkle fish with salt and pepper and place skin side down in a shallow baking pan. Combine remaining ingredients and pour over fish. Refrigerate, covered, turning occasionally, for one hour.

Grill fish skin side up 4 inches from hot coals for 3 to 4 minutes, basting with marinade. Flip fillets and cook an additional 2 to 3 minutes, until the flesh is opaque all the way through and the top surface has a light golden crust. Serve with hot mango sauce.

Yield: 4 servings.

Hot Mango Sauce

1 Brooks mango
1 Brooks scotch bonnet pepper, seeds and ribs removed
$1/2$ cup chicken broth, either homemade or low-sodium canned
$1/4$ teaspoon Brooks ginger root, grated
$1/2$ tablespoon honey
Salt and freshly ground pepper to taste

Cut the mango on both sides of the pit. Reserve a few slices for decoration. Scoop out all the rest of the flesh and purée in a blender or food processor fitted with the steel blade. Add the scotch bonnet pepper, chicken broth, ginger root and honey. Blend until smooth.

Pour the mixture into a medium-size saucepan and heat on medium-low for about 8 minutes. Season with salt and pepper and serve hot over the grilled fish.

Yield: 4 servings.

From the Florida Grill

Turn your next backyard barbecue
into a Floribbean adventure!

Avocado and Tomato Salad with Lime Vinaigrette

Barbecued Shrimp with
Hot Mango Sauce *page 38*

Curried Rice*

Raspberry Sherbet*

*indicates menu suggestions for which there are no recipes

Avocado and Tomato Salad

1 Brooks Big-Un avocado, peeled and pitted
2 ripe tomatoes
3 chopped scallions (green onions)
Lime Vinaigrette

Slice avocado and quarter tomatoes. Arrange on serving dish with chopped scallions. Top with Lime Vinaigrette.

Yield: 4 servings.

Lime Vinaigrette

1 clove garlic, crushed
$^1/_2$ teaspoon salt
$^1/_2$ teaspoon Dijon-style mustard
3 tablespoons fresh lime juice
1$^1/_2$ tablespoons Grand Marnier or other orange liqueur
$^3/_4$ cup olive oil

Using a fork, mash garlic and salt to a paste in a small bowl. Stir in mustard, lime juice, and Grand Marnier.

Gradually whisk in olive oil until mixture is smooth and thick. Adjust the flavor by adding more lime juice or olive oil if needed.

Yield: 1 cup.

Barbecued Shrimp

1 pound extra large shrimp
¹/₂ pound cachucha peppers
2 Brooks fresh limes, quartered
Hot Mango Sauce

Choose the very largest shrimp you can find. Peel, then split them with a knife, removing the vein. Wash thoroughly. String shrimp on small skewers, alternating them with the peppers.

Broil over very hot charcoal or on the electric grill for 3 to 5 minutes. Serve hot, using Hot Mango Sauce (see page 38) to dunk the shrimp. Garnish with lime quarters.

Yield: 4 servings.

South Beach Fare

Try Florida Avocado and Crab Salad for an ultra cool summertime luncheon.

Brooks Florida Avocado and Crab Meat Salad

Parmesan Breadsticks*

Angel Star Cakes Crowned
with Tropical Fruit Compote

*indicates menu suggestions for which there are no recipes

Brooks Florida Avocado and Crab Meat Salad

This cool salad is good year-round but seems most appropriate during summer. As a variation you may substitute cooked shrimp for the crab meat.

Juice of 3 Brooks limes
1 teaspoon Dijon mustard
$^1/_4$ teaspoon salt
$^1/_8$ teaspoon freshly ground pepper
$^1/_2$ cup olive oil
1 pound lump or backfin crab meat, picked over carefully to remove
    any stray cartilage
2 medium Brooks avocados
$^1/_2$ teaspoon lime zest
Chopped parsley and red caviar for garnish

Combine lime juice, mustard, salt and pepper in a small mixing bowl. Gradually whisk in olive oil until smooth and blended. Pour over the crab meat and let stand for 10 minutes.

Drain excess dressing from crab meat. Just before serving, cut avocados in half. Remove and discard pits. Cut avocados into thin slices. Mound the crab meat in the center of a serving platter. Arrange avocado slices in a fan shape around the crab meat. Sprinkle with lime zest, chopped parsley, and red caviar.

Yield: 4 servings.

Angel Star Cakes Crowned with Tropical Fruit Compote

Cakes
½ cup cake flour
2 tablespoons plus ⅓ cup sugar
6 large egg whites
Pinch of cream of tartar
Pinch of salt
½ teaspoon vanilla extract

Compote
2 cups cubed star fruit
1 cup cubed banana
1 cup cubed kiwifruit
1 cup cubed mango
3 tablespoons fresh lime juice
1 tablespoon sugar

Preheat oven to 350 degrees. Sift cake flour and 2 tablespoons sugar into medium bowl. Using electric mixer, beat egg whites in large bowl until foamy. Add cream of tartar and salt and beat until soft peaks form. Gradually add remaining ⅓ cup sugar, beating until whites are stiff. Beat in vanilla. Sift dry ingredients over whites. Using rubber spatula, gently fold into whites just until incorporated.

Quickly rinse six 10-ounce custard cups or ramekins with cold water and arrange on cookie sheet. Divide batter among cups; smooth tops. Bake until cakes are puffed, light golden and tester inserted into center of each cake comes out clean, about 15 minutes. Transfer cups to rack and cool. (Can be made 3 hours ahead. Let stand at room temperature.)

Combine all fruit in bowl. Mix in lime juice and sugar. (Can be made 3 hours ahead. Cover and chill. Serve at room temperature.) Loosen sides of cakes with small knife and turn onto plates. Surround cakes with compote and serve.

Yield: 6 servings.

Tropical Picnic

Picnic with Floribbean flair!

Chef Tony's Chayote Tropical Salad

Grilled Papaya-Ginger Chicken

Yuca Shoestrings *page 91*

Tropical Salsa

Corn on the Cob*

Red or Yellow Watermelon Wedges*

Assorted Microbrew Beers*

*indicates menu suggestions for which there are no recipes

Chef Tony's Chayote Tropical Salad

Refreshing strips of chayote add just the right crunch to this colorful salad.

2 Brooks chayotes, peeled, and cut into julienne
1 large red onion, chopped
1 Brooks papaya, peeled, seeded, and cubed
3 Brooks clementines, segmented (or other sweet citrus)
Salt to taste
Clementine zest or other sweet citrus zest
1/4 cup balsamic vinegar
1/8 cup water
1/2 tablespoon Italian seasoning
1/4 teaspoon Brooks fresh ginger root, grated
1/2 cup olive oil

Mix chayotes, onion, papaya, clementines and salt in a large bowl.

In a small bowl, mix clementine zest, vinegar, water, Italian seasoning, ginger root and oil together. Add to chayote mixture and stir. Refrigerate for 1 hour before serving.

Yield: 6 servings.

Tropical Salsa

1 Florida avocado, halved, and chopped small (about 1/4 inch)
4 plum tomatoes, diced
3 scallions or green onions, sliced (about 1/3 cup)
1/4 cup chopped cilantro, or parsley
1 scotch bonnet pepper, seeded and minced (about 1 tablespoon)
1 teaspoon dried, crumbled oregano
1/4 cup fresh lime juice
2 tablespoons olive oil
Salt and pepper to taste

Toss avocado, tomatoes, scallions, cilantro, pepper and oregano in a medium-size bowl. Add lime juice and olive oil, stirring to coat. Season with salt and pepper. Best if prepared just before serving.

Yield: 2 cups.

Grilled Papaya-Ginger Chicken Barbecue Sauce

1/2 Sunrise Solo Papaya, peeled, seeded and sliced
2 tablespoons freshly grated ginger
2 1/2 cups orange juice

Reserve a few papaya slices for decoration. Purée remaining papaya, grated ginger and orange juice in a blender or food processor fitted with the steel blade until smooth. Baste chicken during the last 10 minutes on the grill.

Yield: 3 cups.

Summer Sizzler

Sautéed chicken breasts with tropical fruit salsa are sure to become a summertime favorite.

Fresh Spinach and Wild Mushroom Salad*

Floribbean Chicken with Papaya Salsa

or

Papaya-Lychee Salsa for Red Snapper

Yuca Shoestrings page 91

Minted Papaya Wedges*

*indicates menu suggestions for which there are no recipes

Floribbean Chicken with Papaya Salsa

Boneless chicken breasts are quick and economical to serve. This chicken has a crisp golden crust and the zing of fresh lime. It's good hot and terrific cold, especially on a picnic.

1 egg
1/2 cup Brooks fresh lime juice
1 1/2 cups cornflake crumbs or plain bread crumbs
1/2 teaspoon salt
1/4 teaspoon freshly ground pepper
3 tablespoons olive oil
1 tablespoon butter
4 boneless, skinless chicken breast halves
Papaya Salsa

In a shallow bowl, lightly beat egg and lime juice together. Combine bread crumbs and salt and pepper in a shallow bowl. Heat the oil and butter in a large sauté pan until hot. Dip the chicken breasts in the egg mixture and let the excess drain off. Coat with crumbs, shaking off the excess.

Sauté the chicken over moderate heat until golden on both sides, about 4 to 5 minutes on each side. Transfer to paper towels and let drain. Place chicken on serving plates. Add Papaya Salsa to the sauté pan and heat for 2 minutes. Spoon Papaya Salsa over chicken breasts.

Yield: 8 servings.

Papaya Salsa

1 ripe Brooks papaya, peeled and seeded
1 small red bell pepper
1 small red onion
1 Brooks scotch bonnet pepper
6 tablespoons Brooks fresh limes
¼ cup pineapple juice
¼ cup fresh cilantro
Salt and pepper to taste

Dice the papaya, red pepper and red onion. Using rubber gloves, finely mince the Brooks scotch bonnet pepper. Combine with remaining ingredients in a medium bowl.

Yield: 3 cups.

Papaya-Lychee Salsa

2 cups diced peeled papaya
11-ounce lychee, diced
½ cup chopped fresh cilantro
½ cup chopped red bell pepper
¼ cup chopped red onion
¼ cup fresh lime juice

Mix all ingredients in bowl. Season to taste with salt and pepper. Cover and refrigerate until ready to use. (Can be prepared 4 hours ahead.)

Yield: 4½ cups.

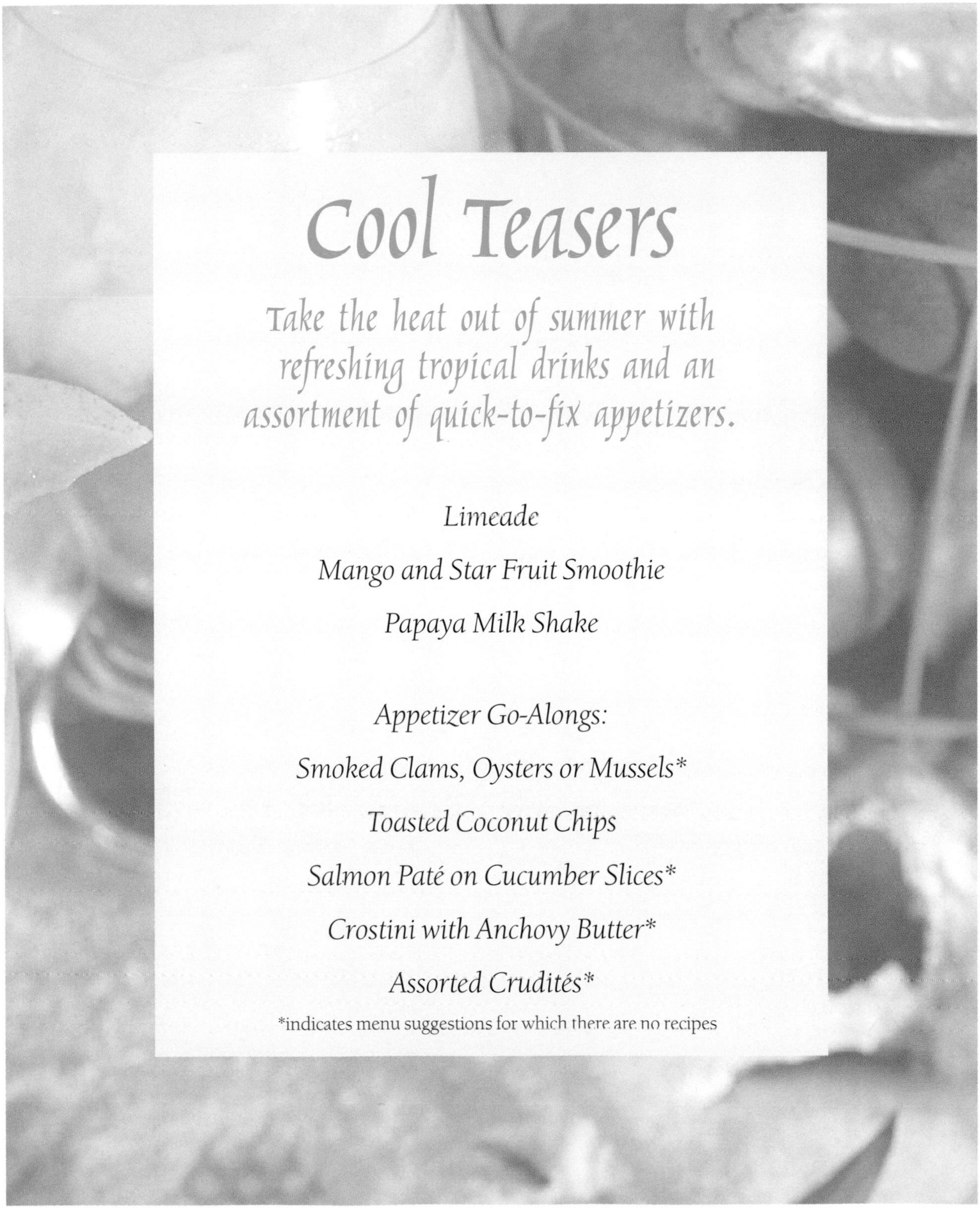

Cool Teasers

Take the heat out of summer with refreshing tropical drinks and an assortment of quick-to-fix appetizers.

Limeade

Mango and Star Fruit Smoothie

Papaya Milk Shake

Appetizer Go-Alongs:

Smoked Clams, Oysters or Mussels*

Toasted Coconut Chips

Salmon Paté on Cucumber Slices*

Crostini with Anchovy Butter*

Assorted Crudités*

*indicates menu suggestions for which there are no recipes

Limeade

Chill out with this ice-cold limeade made with Brooks limes. It's the most refreshing drink to serve at summertime festivities.

3 cups water
3/4 cup sugar
1 cup fresh lime juice, chilled
Lime slices for garnish

Combine water and sugar in a medium saucepan. Bring to a boil and cook over medium heat until sugar is dissolved. Remove from heat and cool for about 20 minutes. Pour sugar syrup into a pitcher and chill. Add chilled lime juice to pitcher and stir well. Serve over ice and garnish with lime slices.

Yield: 1 quart.

Papaya Milk Shake

3 Brooks papayas, peeled, seeded and diced
1 ripe banana, diced
3/4 cup milk
1/4 cup heavy cream
1 cup crushed ice

In a blender, purée the papaya, banana, milk, cream and crushed ice. Pour into four tall glasses and serve.

Yield: 4 servings.

Toasted Coconut Chips

Coconut chips are usually eaten as a snack, but work well as an appetizer also. Spices such as curry or ground hot pepper may be added with salt for extra flavor. When selecting a coconut, choose one that sloshes when shaken and whose "eyes" are free from decay. Save the coconut water to drink or use in dessert recipes.

1 coconut
Salt to taste

Preheat oven to 350 degrees. Puncture "eyes" of the coconut with a screwdriver or other strong, sharp object. Drain liquid into a container to save for future use. Bake whole coconut for 20 minutes. Crack shell with a few taps of a hammer. Pry meat away from shell, using a blunt-edged knife to separate if necessary. Using narrowest slicing blade of a food processor available, cut coconut chunks to form the longest possible slices. Arrange these in a single layer on a cookie sheet. Bake for 10 to 12 minutes or until light golden brown. Immediately sprinkle with salt. Cool and serve. May be stored in a sealed plastic container.

Yield: 3 cups.

Mango and Star Fruit Smoothie

The exotic taste of this quenching cooler is irresistible.

8 ounces plain yogurt, drained
1 cup fresh orange juice
3 large Brooks star fruit
2 large Brooks mangoes, peeled and seeded

In a blender, purée all ingredients until smooth. Chill.

Yield: 6 to 8 cups.

59

Floribbean Fall

Tropical fruits and vegetables are plentiful right through fall. Cooking with tropicals is as colorful as a forest in autumn.

Autumn Supper

Complement a hardy autumn supper
with a refreshing Latino-style salad.

Avocado, Papaya and Hearts of Palm Salad

Lime Vinaigrette page 42

Grilled Lamb Chops*

or

Sautéed Shrimp and Star Fruit

Barley Pilaf*

Blackberry Cobbler*

*indicates menu suggestions for which there are no recipes

Avocado, Papaya and Hearts of Palm Salad

This unusual tropical salad tastes as good as it looks. It makes a good first course arranged on lettuce leaves, or a good accompaniment to simple grilled chicken, beef or lamb.

1 Brooks papaya, peeled, seeded and cut into ¹/₂-inch cubes
1 Brooks avocado, peeled, pitted and cut into 1-inch cubes
1 can (14 ounces) hearts of palm, drained, rinsed and cut on the diagonal
1 ripe tomato, cut into ¹/₂-inch cubes
into ¹/₂-inch pieces
Salt and pepper to taste
Lime Vinaigrette (see page 42)
¹/₄ cup julienne strips of Brooks chayote for garnish

Combine papaya, avocado, hearts of palm, and tomato in a large bowl. Season with salt and pepper. Sprinkle with Lime Vinaigrette and toss gently. Refrigerate, covered, for 1 hour.

Divide this mixture on salad plates. Garnish with chayote strips.

Yield: 4 servings.

Sautéed Shrimp and Star Fruit

1 pound shrimp, preferably small
3 small star fruit, preferably medium-sweet, about 2 ounces each
2¹/₂ tablespoons butter (divided use)
Salt and white pepper to taste
Pinch of sugar
1¹/₂ tablespoons lime juice

Shell and devein shrimp. If they're not small, half lengthwise. Cut tips off the star fruit, then slice ¹/₈ inch thick. Heat 2 tablespoons butter in large nonstick sauté pan. Add shrimp, star fruit slices, salt, pepper and sugar. Sauté for a minute or two, until shrimp are pink. Add lime juice and toss. Remove from heat; stir in remaining butter. Taste and season. Serve at once.

Yield: 2 servings.

Bouillabaisse Dinner

This tropical version of classic bouillabaisse is bound to become a culinary hit.

Spinach-Avocado Salad with
Tequila Lime Dressing

Floribbean Bouillabaisse

Crusty French Bread*

Spumoni Ice Cream*

*indicates menu suggestions for which there are no recipes

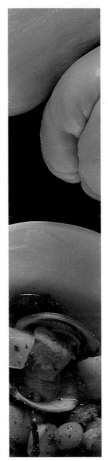

Floribbean Bouillabaisse

The freshest catch of the day is transformed in this zesty fish soup. Crusty bread, a green salad and a simple dessert are all you need to complete the meal.

3 tablespoons olive oil
1 sweet onion, chopped
3 cloves garlic, finely chopped
1 teaspoon Brooks fresh ginger root, finely chopped
1 carrot, peeled and diced
1 Brooks chayote squash, peeled and diced
1 Brooks malanga, peeled and diced
3 large tomatoes, peeled, seeded and chopped
¼ bunch cilantro, finely chopped
3 bay leaves
1 tablespoon fresh Brooks lime juice
8 ounces star fruit wine or dry white wine
3 cups chicken broth
2 cups clam juice
18 baby clams, scrubbed
12 mussels, scrubbed
1 pound mixed firm-fleshed fish (red snapper, yellowtail, tuna, or
    monkfish), cut into 2-inch pieces
8 ounces scallops
12 ounces shrimp, peeled, deveined, tail on

Heat olive oil in a large pot over medium heat. Stir in onion, garlic and ginger root. Cook until softened, about 5 minutes. Add carrot, chayote, malanga, tomatoes, cilantro, bay leaves and lime juice. Simmer until blended, about 8 minutes.

Add wine, chicken broth and clam juice and bring to a boil; lower heat to medium and add clams and mussels to the broth. Simmer until clams and mussels open, 5 to 7 minutes; discard any that have not opened. Add mixed fish, scallops and shrimp and simmer 4 minutes longer or until shrimp are bright pink and scallops and fish are firm. Season with salt and pepper.

Yield: 6 servings.

Spinach-Avocado Salad with Tequila Lime Dressing

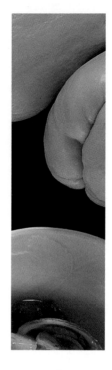

8 ounces jicama or radishes
2 ripe Florida avocados, peeled, seeded and thinly sliced
2 tablespoons fresh lime juice
1½ pounds (10 cups) fresh spinach, rinsed, dried, stemmed
1 medium red onion, thinly sliced
½ cup sweetened dried cranberries (optional)

Make Tequila Lime Dressing. Pare/peel jicama or trim radishes: cut into 1x¼-inch strips. Gently toss avocados with lime juice in mixing bowl.

Place spinach, avocados, onion, and jicama in large salad bowl. Drizzle salad with dressing and toss gently to coat. Garnish with dried cranberries.

Yield: 8 servings.

Tequila Lime Dressing

½ cup olive oil
2 tablespoons tequila
2 tablespoons fresh lime juice
1 tablespoon chopped fresh coriander
1 teaspoon sugar
½ teaspoon salt
¼ teaspoon ground cumin
¼ teaspoon freshly ground pepper

Whisk all ingredients together in small bowl or shake in jar with tight-fitting lid.

Fall Soups

Tropical soups make flavorful fall dining.

Cream of Chayote Soup with
Toasted Pumpkin Seeds

Calabaza Soup

Avocado and Tomato Slices*

Corn Muffins*

Fresh Pineapple Spears*

*indicates menu suggestions for which there are no recipes

Cream of Chayote Soup with Toasted Pumpkin Seeds

This rich, elegant soup is a perfect beginning for a memorable dinner.

2 tablespoons unsalted butter
1/4 cup chopped onion
1/2 cup chopped celery
4 Brooks chayotes, peeled and coarsely chopped
6 cups homemade or low-sodium canned chicken broth
Salt and pepper to taste
2 cups heavy cream or half-and-half
1 teaspoon fresh lime juice
1/4 cup toasted pumpkin seeds
2 teaspoons chopped fresh dill

Melt butter in a large saucepan over medium heat. Add onion and celery and sauté, stirring until the vegetables are soft and golden, about 5 minutes.

Add the chayotes, chicken broth, and salt and pepper to taste. Bring to a boil, then reduce heat, cover, and simmer until chayotes are tender, about 25 minutes.

Pour the soup through a strainer and transfer the solids to a bowl or a food processor fitted with the steel blade, or use a food mill. Add 1 cup of the cooking liquid and process until smooth. Return purée to the pot and add enough of the remaining cooking liquid to make soup the desired consistency. Stir to combine and bring soup to a boil.

Add heavy cream or half-and-half and simmer until slightly thickened. Season with lime juice. To serve, garnish with pumpkin seeds and dill.

Yield: 6 to 8 servings.

Calabaza Soup

This light, colorful soup is particularly appropriate for the holidays, but it's good and easy to prepare year-round.

2 tablespoons unsalted butter
1 large sweet onion, minced
3 scallions, trimmed and minced
1 (3-pound) Brooks calabaza, peeled, cleaned and chopped into 1-inch cubes
2 carrots, peeled and coarsely chopped
8 cups homemade or low-sodium canned chicken broth
Salt and freshly ground black pepper to taste
Pinch of cayenne pepper
Herb Bouquet: 1 sprig thyme, 2 sprigs parsley, 1 bay leaf tied together
2 Brooks mangoes, peeled, seeded and coarsely chopped
Juice of 1 Brooks lime
Sour cream or plain yogurt for garnish
Chopped parsley for garnish

Melt butter in a large saucepan over medium heat. Add onion and scallions and sauté, stirring until the onion mixture is soft and golden, about 5 minutes.

Add the calabaza, carrots, chicken broth, salt and pepper to taste, and pinch of cayenne pepper.

Add herb bouquet to saucepan. Bring to a boil, then reduce heat, cover, and simmer until vegetables are tender, about 40 minutes.

Remove the herb bouquet and pour the soup through a strainer and transfer the solids to the bowl of a food processor fitted with the steel blade, or use a food mill. Add the mangoes and 1 cup of the cooking liquid and process until smooth.

Return purée to the pot and add remaining cooking liquid. Stir to combine and bring soup to a boil. Season with lime juice.

To serve, top with sour cream or yogurt and garnish with chopped parsley.

Yield: 6 to 8 servings.

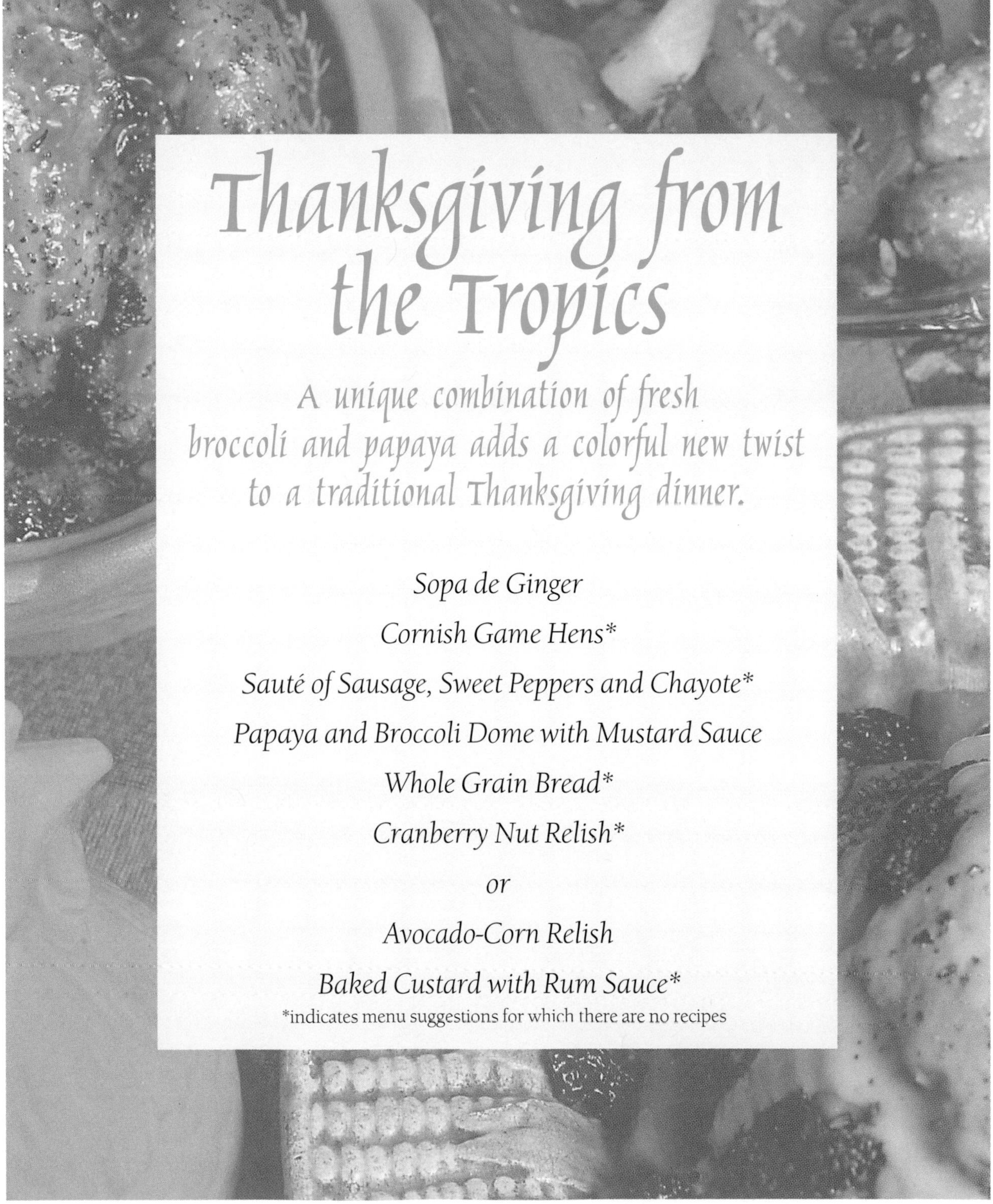

Thanksgiving from the Tropics

A unique combination of fresh broccoli and papaya adds a colorful new twist to a traditional Thanksgiving dinner.

Sopa de Ginger

Cornish Game Hens*

Sauté of Sausage, Sweet Peppers and Chayote*

Papaya and Broccoli Dome with Mustard Sauce

Whole Grain Bread*

Cranberry Nut Relish*

or

Avocado-Corn Relish

Baked Custard with Rum Sauce*

*indicates menu suggestions for which there are no recipes

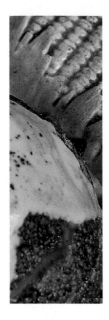

Papaya and Broccoli Dome with Mustard Sauce

This colorful presentation of broccoli may be served either at room temperature or cold.

2 quarts water
1 tablespoon salt
2 pounds broccoli, cut into florets
2 Brooks Sunrise papayas, peeled, seeded and sliced
Salt to taste

Bring water to a boil in a large pot. Add salt and broccoli. Return water to a boil, covering the pan so that the water returns to the boil rapidly. Boil, uncovered, for 4 to 5 minutes or until tender. Drain and plunge immediately into cold water to retain the bright green color; drain, and pat dry. Line a stainless steel bowl, about 8 inches wide and 5 inches deep, with alternating rings of broccoli and papaya. Start with a layer of broccoli (flowered side against the bowl and stems pointing in). Then ring a row of papaya slices. Continue to alternate broccoli and papaya, pressing down slightly as you layer them, until the bowl is full. Fill the center with smaller pieces. As you fill it, sprinkle the center with salt. Press down with a weighted plate. After 15 minutes, tip to drain liquid from the bowl. Remove the weighted plate and place a serving plate on the bowl. Reverse carefully, and unmold. Pour Mustard Sauce on top and garnish with a papaya slice. Ring the serving platter with papaya slices.

Yield: 6 servings.

Mustard Sauce

This sauce is excellent with grilled salmon or as a dipping sauce for stone crabs.

$1/2$ cup Dijon mustard
2 tablespoons sugar
$1/4$ cup white wine vinegar
$3/4$ cup extra-virgin olive oil
4 to 5 tablespoons water

In a bowl, whisk together mustard, sugar and vinegar until sugar is dissolved. Whisk in oil until sauce is smooth. Whisk in water to thin sauce to desired consistency.

Sopa de Ginger

6 tablespoons (³/4 stick) butter
2¹/2 pounds beets, peeled, diced
1 large onion, chopped
1 (8-ounce) russet potato, peeled, chopped
5 cups low-salt chicken broth
1¹/2 tablespoons minced fresh ginger
¹/4 cup whipping cream

Melt butter in heavy large saucepan over medium-high heat. Add beets, onion and potato; sauté for 10 minutes. Add broth and ginger; bring to simmer. Reduce heat; cover and simmer until vegetables are very soft, about 1 hour. Working in batches, transfer soup to blender and purée. Season with salt and pepper. (May be made 1 day ahead. Cover and chill.) Rewarm soup. Ladle into bowls and drizzle with cream.

Yield: 6 to 8 servings.

Avocado-Corn Relish

12 ounces plum tomatoes, seeded, chopped
1 large Florida avocado, peeled, diced
³/4 cup fresh corn kernels or frozen, thawed
¹/3 cup chopped sweet red onion
3 tablespoons chopped fresh cilantro
2 tablespoons fresh lime juice
¹/8 to ¹/4 teaspoon dried crushed red pepper

Combine all ingredients in medium bowl and stir gently to blend. Season to taste with salt and pepper. Cover and refrigerate for up to 3 hours.

Yield: 3¹/2 cups.

Florida Favorites

Uniq fruit and fennel create
a stunning first course salad for this
autumn supper menu.

Uniq Fruit and Fennel Salad with
Lime Vinaigrette page 42

Salmon in Lime-Ginger Sauce

Calabacitas

Sautéed Bananas with Brandy*

*indicates menu suggestions for which there are no recipes

Uniq Fruit and Fennel Salad

Thin slices of fennel combine with the citrus flavor of Uniq fruit in a tangy vinaigrette for a refreshing fall salad.

40 spinach leaves, cleaned and stemmed
4 Brooks Uniq fruit, peeled and sectioned
1 fennel bulb, cleaned, quartered and thinly sliced
2 ripe medium tomatoes, cored, seeded, and cubed

Arrange 10 washed and patted dry spinach leaves on 4 individual salad plates. Place Uniq sections in a pinwheel on the spinach leaves. Sprinkle thinly sliced fennel in center of salad. Place 1 tablespoon cubed tomato between each Uniq fruit section. Dress with Lime Vinaigrette.

Yield: 4 servings.

Calabacitas

2 tablespoons olive oil
1 cup chopped sweet onion
2 chayote squash, cubed (about 1 pound)
1 clove garlic, minced
2 yellow or red bell peppers, stemmed, seeded, cut into $^1/_4$-inch strips
$^1/_2$ scotch bonnet pepper, stemmed, seeded and minced
1 cup coarsely chopped fresh plum tomatoes
Salt and freshly ground pepper to taste
1 cup grated sharp Cheddar cheese (about 4 ounces)

Heat oil in large skillet over medium heat until rippling. Add onion and sauté for 2 minutes. Add chayote and sauté until lightly browned, about 8 to 10 minutes. Add garlic; sauté for 1 minute. Add bell peppers, scotch bonnet, and tomatoes. Cook, stirring juices, about 2 to 3 minutes. Season with salt and pepper and stir in cheese. Serve hot.

Yield: 8 servings.

Salmon in Lime-Ginger Sauce

¼ cup chopped fresh cilantro
3 tablespoons chopped fresh ginger
2 tablespoons coarsely chopped garlic
1 scotch bonnet pepper, seeded and coarsely chopped
1 red bell pepper, seeded and coarsely chopped
3 tablespoons fresh lime juice
1 tablespoons vegetable oil, preferably canola oil
½ teaspoon salt
¼ teaspoon turmeric
1¼ pounds salmon or halibut fillet, cut into 2x2-inch pieces

Using a food processor or a mortar and pestle, grind together cilantro, ginger, garlic and peppers until a relatively smooth paste results, adding a little water if necessary. Add lime juice, oil, salt and turmeric and mix well. Toss the fish pieces in this marinade in a shallow dish, making sure each piece is well coated. Cover and refrigerate for 5 to 10 minutes. Coat the bottom of a large skillet with 3 to 4 tablespoons of the marinade. Transfer the fish pieces to the skillet and cover with the remaining marinade. Cover the skillet with a tight-fitting lid and place over medium-low heat. Cook gently until the interior of the fish is opaque, 5 to 10 minutes. (Cooking time will vary with the thickness of the fillet.)

Yield: 4 servings.

Spice Up Autumn with Hot Flavors

*Move over Tex-Mex...
here comes Caribbean Chili!*

Mixed Greens Salad*

Caribbean Chili

or

Grilled Swordfish with Papaya Salsa

Mango-Tomato Salsa

Boniato Corn Fritters

Lemon Bars*

*indicates menu suggestions for which there are no recipes

Caribbean Chili

Some like it hot; others like it mild. Just keep adding red pepper sauce a little at a time until it tastes right to you. Chili can be made days in advance.

1 tablespoon vegetable oil
2 medium onions, chopped
1 red bell pepper, chopped
4 carrots, peeled and sliced
1 Brooks chayote squash, peeled and chopped
3 stalks celery, chopped
4 cloves garlic, finely chopped
1 pound "hot" turkey sausage, removed from casing
1 tablespoon dried oregano
3 tablespoons chili powder
1 teaspoon red pepper (Tabasco) sauce
$1/2$ teaspoon red pepper flakes
1 teaspoon sugar
Juice from one Brooks lime
1 (28-ounce) can crushed tomatoes
1 (15-ounce) can tomato sauce
1 (14$1/2$-ounce) can whole tomatoes, drained
1 cup chicken broth, either homemade or canned
Salt and pepper to taste
3 (16-ounce) cans red kidney beans, rinsed and drained
1 pound frozen corn kernels
1 (6-ounce) can pitted green olives, drained and sliced
Sour cream, chopped scallions, grated Cheddar cheese, shredded Brooks
    chayote, chopped cilantro, wedges of Brooks limes, homemade or
    bottled salsa for garnish

Heat oil in a 12-inch skillet over medium-high heat. Add onions, bell pepper, carrots, chayote squash, celery and garlic; cook for 5 minutes, stirring frequently until vegetables are almost tender. Add sausage and sauté for about 5 minutes, stirring frequently until meat has lost its raw look. Stir in oregano, chili powder, red pepper sauce, red pepper flakes, sugar and lime juice and sauté for 2 minutes. Add remaining ingredients and bring to a boil. Reduce heat and simmer, uncovered, for 30 minutes, stirring occasionally until mixture is thickened. Season to taste with salt and pepper and more red pepper sauce if desired. Ladle into bowls. Serve with sour cream, scallions, cheese, chayote, cilantro, limes and salsa.

Yield: 6 servings.

Grilled Swordfish with Papaya Salsa

2 large papaya, peeled, seeded, cut into $^1/_2$-inch dice
9 ounces red onions, peeled, diced
6 ounces red bell peppers, cored, seeded, diced
1$^1/_2$ ounces mint leaves, chopped
5 tablespoons lime juice
3 tablespoons scotch bonnet pepper, seeded and minced
3 tablespoons raspberry vinegar
Salt to taste
4 (6-ounce) swordfish steaks
Canola oil
Freshly ground black pepper to taste

Combine papaya, onion, bell pepper, mint, lime juice, scotch bonnet pepper and vinegar. Season with salt. Cover: refrigerate. For each serving, lightly brush 1 fillet with oil; sprinkle with salt and pepper. Grill for about 10 minutes or until opaque, turning once. Remove fillet to a plate; top with $^1/_2$ cup salsa.

Yield: 24 servings.

Mango-Tomato Salsa

2 ripe mangoes
1 large tomato, peeled and cubed
1/2 cup minced onion (white, red or green)
1 large red or yellow bell pepper, seeded and finely chopped
1 tablespoon habanero (scotch bonnet) pepper, seeded and finely
    chopped
1 lime, juiced
1 tablespoon sugar
1 teaspoon salt
Chopped fresh cilantro to taste

Peel mangoes and remove flesh. Chop coarsely in a food processor or by hand. Transfer mangoes to bowl and stir in remaining ingredients. Mix well. The adventurous can add an additional seeded chopped habanero pepper or 1/2 teaspoon chili oil.

Yield: about 3 cups.

Boniato Corn Fritters

Boniato fritters made with sweet potato, corn and a little grated ginger make an earthy companion dish.

4 large (about 3 pounds) Boniato potatoes, peeled and rinsed
1 small onion, peeled
2 eggs
1 (7^{1}/2-ounce) can whole kernel corn
^{1}/3 cup all-purpose flour
1 teaspoon fresh ginger root, grated
2 teaspoons salt
^{1}/8 teaspoon pepper
^{1}/3 cup olive oil

Coarsely shred potatoes and small onion into large bowl half filled with water. Drain shredded potatoes and onion in a colander lined with a clean towel or cheesecloth. Wrap potatoes and onion in towel; squeeze towel to remove as much water as possible. In the same large bowl, beat eggs; add the shredded potatoes, onion, corn, flour, ginger root, salt and pepper and toss together until well mixed. Heat olive oil in a 12-inch skillet over medium heat until hot; drop mixture by scant ^{1}/4 cupfuls into 4 mounds.

Flatten each mound with spatula to make a 4-inch fritter.

Cook until golden brown on one side, about 4 minutes; turn fritter and brown other side. Remove to paper towel-lined cookie sheet to drain; keep warm. Repeat until all the mixture is used.

Yield: 16 to 18 fritters.

Floribbean Winter

Warm up winter with hearty
vegetables and succulent fruits.
Enjoy a taste of the tropics.

Winter Fest

Ring in the New Year
with a Floribbean-inspired feast.

Tropical Fruit Salad

Steamed Chicken Breasts with Chayote
Mango Sauce

Chayote and Wild Rice Waffles

Taro or Yuca Root Shoestrings

French Vanilla Ice Cream with Brandied Fruit*

*indicates menu suggestions for which there are no recipes

Tropical Fruit Salad

2 cups seedless red grapes
1 cup (1-inch) cubed, peeled ripe papaya
1 cup sliced star fruit
3 kiwifruit peeled, halved lengthwise and sliced (about 1 cup)
3 tablespoons fresh lime juice
2 tablespoons honey
1 1/4 cups sliced ripe banana

Combine first 4 ingredients in a bowl; toss gently. Combine lime juice and honey in a small bowl, stirring with a wire whisk until blended. Pour over fruit; toss gently to coat. Cover and chill. Before serving, add banana; toss gently.

Mix everything except the bananas up to 4 hours ahead so the flavors can blend. Add the bananas just before serving.

Yield: six 1-cup servings.

Steamed Chicken Breasts with Chayote

Steaming produces a very delicate and low-fat chicken main dish accented by a spicy mango sauce.

2 scallions, sliced
1 carrot, peeled and cut into julienne
1 Brooks chayote, peeled and cut into julienne
4 skinless, boneless chicken breast halves
Salt and freshly ground pepper to taste

Place scallions, carrot, and chayote in a medium-size mixing bowl and mix together. Slice the chicken breasts open lengthwise without cutting through (like an open book). Season with salt and pepper. Cover half of each chicken breast with the vegetables. Fold the top half of the breast over the stuffing. Seal in the stuffing by pressing the two edges together. Season with salt and pepper. Place the chicken breast in a steamer for about 15 minutes or until the chicken is cooked through. Serve with hot mango sauce.

Yield: 4 servings.

Mango Sauce

Don't rub your eyes or touch your face when handling chile peppers and wash your hands thoroughly when you are done.

1 Brooks mango
1 jalapeño pepper, seeds and ribs removed
$1/2$ cup chicken broth, either homemade or low-sodium canned
$1/4$ teaspoon Brooks ginger root, grated
$1/2$ tablespoon honey
Salt and freshly ground pepper to taste

Cut the mango on both sides of the pit. Reserve a few slices for decoration. Scoop out all the rest of the flesh and purée in a blender or food processor fitted with the steel blade. Add the jalapeño pepper, chicken broth, ginger root and honey. Blend until smooth. Pour the mixture into a medium-size saucepan and heat on medium-low for about 8 minutes. Season with salt and pepper and serve hot.

Chayote and Wild Rice Waffles

These crispy waffles topped with grilled chicken or swordfish make an outstanding presentation. They may also be cut on an angle and used as a garnish.

5 ounces wild rice and white rice combination with seasonings
1 cup cake flour
2 teaspoons double-acting baking powder
$\frac{1}{2}$ teaspoon salt
3 eggs or egg substitute
5 tablespoons vegetable oil
1$\frac{1}{2}$ cups milk
1 Brooks chayote, cut into thin strips

Cook rice according to package directions; set aside to cool. Preheat a waffle iron and grease it lightly. Combine flour, baking powder, and salt in a large bowl. Add eggs or egg substitute, oil and $\frac{1}{2}$ cup milk. Add rice, chayote, and remaining milk. Combine the batter until smooth. Cook the batter in the prepared waffle iron, using a generous $\frac{1}{3}$ cup for each waffle, until crisp and golden, about 2 minutes. Serve at once.

Yield: about four 5- to 6-inch waffles.

Taro or Yuca Root Shoestrings

Tropical chips can be made from many tropical vegetables, from boniatos to green plantains. For starters, try this version made with taro or yuca

1$\frac{1}{2}$ pounds taro or yuca root
3 to 4 cups canola oil
Salt and black pepper to taste

Peel the taro or yuca root and cut into very thin strips, no more than $\frac{3}{16}$ inch thick. Place the strips in ice water for $\frac{1}{2}$ hour. Dry the strips on paper towels. Pour the oil to a depth of 2 to 3 inches in a deep-fat fryer, wok, or deep heavy skillet and heat to 350 degrees. Fry the shoestrings until golden brown, about 2 minutes, turning with a wire skimmer. Remove shoestrings with the skimmer and drain the chips on paper towels. Sprinkle with salt and pepper and serve at once.

Yield: 6 servings.

Biscayne Bay Days

Add a little Florida sunshine to cold-weather dining with a tropical-style soup and salad combo.

Floribbean Salad

Fiesta Avocado Soup

Sesame Breadsticks*

Coconut Shortbread Cookies

*indicates menu suggestions for which there are no recipes

Floribbean Salad

This colorful tropical salad brings together flavors that are earthy, sweet, and tart making it a terrific first course. The salad is best if you use the most flavorful extra-virgin olive oil you can find.

3 cups cooked black beans, drained
1 cup cooked red beans, drained
1 medium Brooks chayote squash, peeled and diced
1 cup pitted black olives, chopped
2 cups fresh or canned corn kernels, drained
2 red bell peppers, cored, seeded and diced
$\frac{1}{2}$ cup red onion, diced (St. Augustine Sweets)
3 cloves garlic, minced
2 Brooks star fruit, diced
1 Brooks papaya, seeded, peeled and diced
2 Brooks ripe avocados, seeded, peeled and diced
4 tablespoons extra-virgin olive oil
Juice from 1$\frac{1}{2}$ Brooks lime
1 teaspoon balsamic vinegar
1 tablespoon finely chopped cilantro

Stir together beans, chayote, olives, corn, peppers, onion, garlic, star fruit, papaya and avocados in a large bowl. In a separate container, mix together remaining ingredients. Pour over salad mixture and toss.

Yield: 6 servings.

Fiesta Avocado Soup

1 Florida avocado
¼ teaspoon lime juice
¼ cup finely chopped onions
½ cup thinly sliced celery
1 tablespoon butter
1 cup milk
1 cup half & half
1 teaspoon salt
1 hard-cooked egg

Mash avocado in lime juice. Cook onions and celery in butter slowly until tender. Add milk, half & half and salt, and heat to a boil. Remove from heat. Stir in avocado slowly and serve at once. Garnish with a thin slice of avocado topped with seived hard-cooked egg.

Yield: 4 servings.

Coconut Shortbread Cookies

2 sticks (1 cup) unsalted butter, softened
½ cup granulated sugar
¼ cup firmly packed dark brown sugar
½ teaspoon salt
¼ teaspoon vanilla extract
¾ cup fresh coconut
1½ cups all-purpose flour

Cream butter with granulated sugar and brown sugar in a bowl with an electric mixer until mixture is light and fluffy. Add salt, vanilla and ¼ cup of the coconut and beat until combined well. Add flour ¼ cup at a time, beating until mixture is just combined. Divide the dough into 4 balls, roll the balls in the remaining coconut and on each of 2 baking sheets press 2 of the balls into 5 inch rounds. With the tines of a fork, score each round into 6 wedges and prick the edges decoratively. Bake in the middle of a preheated 325-degree oven for 20 to 30 minutes or until just firm. Cut halfway through each round along the prick marks, transfer the shortbread to racks and let cool completely.

Yield: about 24 cookies.

95
Winter

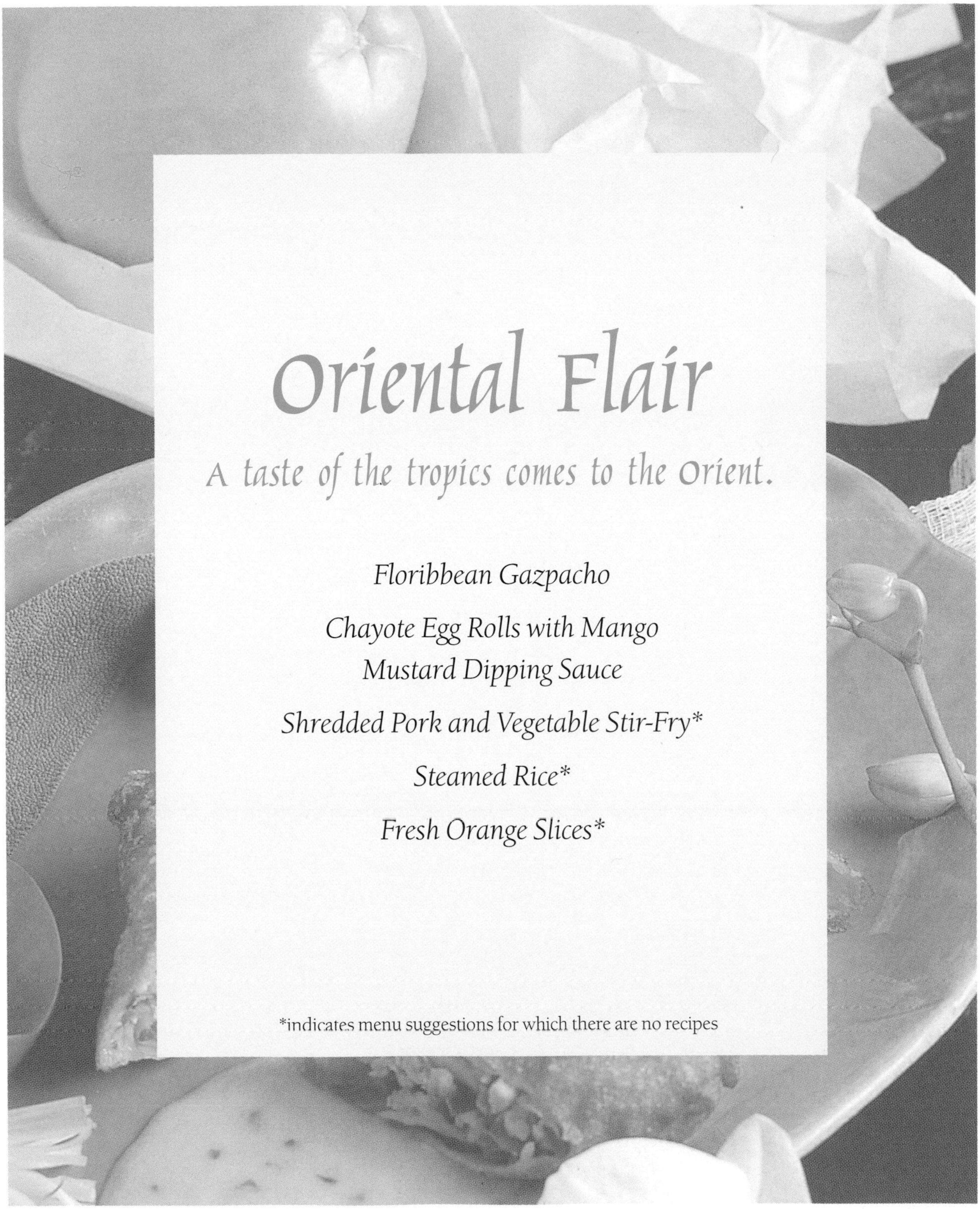

Oriental Flair

A taste of the tropics comes to the Orient.

Floribbean Gazpacho

Chayote Egg Rolls with Mango
Mustard Dipping Sauce

Shredded Pork and Vegetable Stir-Fry*

Steamed Rice*

Fresh Orange Slices*

*indicates menu suggestions for which there are no recipes

Floribbean Gazpacho

3 cups tomato juice
3 cups ripe mango or papaya juice
1 cup cubed peeled fresh pineapple
1 cup cubed peeled semi-ripe papaya
1/2 cup diced red bell pepper
1/2 cup diced green bell pepper
1/2 cup diced yellow bell pepper
1/4 cup fresh lime juice
2 tablespoons chopped fresh coriander
1 teaspoon crushed black pepper
Dash of hot sauce

Combine all ingredients in nonreactive bowl; refrigerate for 4 to 6 hours.
Serve gazpacho in bowls set over crushed ice.

Scale-up: Can be scaled up in direct proportion.

Yield: 8 servings.

Mango Mustard Dipping Sauce

2 Brooks mangoes, peeled, seeded and diced
Juice from 1 Brooks fresh lime
1 tablespoon hot mustard

Process mangoes, lime juice and mustard in a blender or food processor for 30 seconds or
until puréed. Serve with the Chayote Egg Rolls.

Chayote Egg Rolls

Chayote adds crunch to these crispy Oriental appetizers. Egg roll wrappers are available in most supermarkets. For best results fry them just before serving.

5 Brooks chayote squash, peeled and shredded (enough to make 5 cups)
3 carrots, peeled and shredded
1 small onion, chopped
1 teaspoon sugar
$^1/_2$ teaspoon Brooks fresh ginger root, finely chopped
1 tablespoon soy sauce
$^1/_4$ teaspoon toasted sesame oil
$^1/_2$ cup flour
$^1/_4$ cup cornstarch
1 teaspoon baking powder
$^1/_2$ teaspoon baking soda
$^1/_4$ cup water
10 to 12 egg roll or spring roll wrappers
3 cups peanut oil for deep frying
Mango Mustard Dipping Sauce

Blanch chayote, carrots, and onion in boiling water to cover for 15 seconds, drain and refresh under cold running water until cold. Spread out on paper towels to dry. Place in a bowl and toss with remaining ingredients. Combine flour, cornstarch, baking powder, baking soda and water in a bowl and allow to rest, covered and refrigerated, until ready to use.

Divide the egg roll filling into 12 portions. Place the egg roll wrapper pointed side toward you to make a diamond. Put 3 tablespoons filling in the lower third of the wrapper. Bring the bottom of the wrapper up and over the filling, then bring the sides of the wrapper up over the roll to resemble an open envelope. Dip a brush in the batter and paint the flap of the envelope. Continue to roll wrapper until closed. Place flap side down on a baking sheet. Line a baking pan with a paper towel. Heat oil in a wok or heavy saucepan to 375 degrees. Dip each egg roll into batter and place in the oil one by one, adjusting heat to maintain a steady temperature. Add as many egg rolls as can float in one layer on the surface, frying in 2 batches if necessary. Fry until the egg rolls are golden, turning as soon as possible to insure wrapper doesn't open. Fry until golden brown, turning often, about 3 to 4 minutes in all. Remove immediately to drain on the paper towel-lined baking sheet. Serve hot with Mango Mustard Dipping Sauce.

Yield: 12 egg rolls.

¡Feliz Navidad!

Risotto becomes the "star" of the holidays thanks to the addition of beautiful star fruit slices and zesty fresh lime.

Fresh Cranberry Orange Salad*

Roasted Turkey Breast*

Star Fruit Risotto

Sautéed Shredded Boniatos*

Yuca with Garlic

Pound Cake with Fruited Rum Sauce*

*indicates menu suggestions for which there are no recipes

Star Fruit Risotto

Arborio rice absorbs the high proportion of broth and wine used, creates a slightly chewy, nutty-flavored taste, and at the same time produces a creamy consistency. Use a wooden spoon to stir the risotto so you won't damage the tender grains of rice.

2½ quarts chicken broth, either homemade or low-sodium canned
2 tablespoons unsalted butter
2 tablespoons olive oil
2 cups Arborio rice
½ cup star fruit wine or other sweet white wine
¼ cup heavy cream
2 medium Brooks star fruit; one finely chopped and one sliced for garnish
Salt and freshly ground pepper to taste
Zest of 1 Brooks lime for garnish

Bring broth to a simmer in a saucepan and keep it hot for the rest of the cooking time. Heat the butter and oil in a heavy 3-quart casserole over medium-high heat.

Reduce the heat and add the rice and stir to coat it thoroughly with the oil, about 3 minutes. Pour in the wine and let the rice absorb it, stirring to make sure the rice doesn't stick.

Add a ladle full of broth and stir the rice frequently. When the broth has been absorbed, add another ladle full. Stir frequently, adding more broth as required. Never let the pot get too dry. Repeat until the rice is firm but tender, without a chalky center, about 20 minutes. Stir in the heavy cream. Remove from the heat and mix in the chopped star fruit. Season with salt and pepper. Transfer to a greased bowl; pack it firmly. Invert onto a serving plate and garnish with sliced star fruit and a sprinkling of lime zest.

Yield: 6 servings.

Yuca with Garlic

1 medium (1½-pound) yuca
1 teaspoon kosher salt
1 tablespoon (about 3 cloves) garlic, minced
⅓ cup olive oil
⅓ cup fresh lime juice

Using a knife, peel yuca and cut into halves lengthwise. With point of knife, remove center string and chop into bite-size pieces. Combine yuca and salt in a large saucepan and cover with water by 2 to 3 inches. Bring to boil, then lower heat and simmer gently, covered, for about 15 minutes. Meanwhile, combine lime juice, garlic and olive oil in a serving bowl. When yuca is done, drain thoroughly. Toss with lime juice and oil mixture. Serve warm.

Note: Cooking yuca at a hard boil will cause it to break apart.

Yield: 4 servings.

Breakfast in Bed

Breakfast is served...Floribbean style.

Fresh-Squeezed Orange Juice*

Scrambled Eggs with Chopped Chives*

Honey-Baked Ham with Star Fruit Relish

Mango Muffins

Star Fruit, Papaya and Mango Slices*

Sunrise Shake

*indicates menu suggestions for which there are no recipes

Honey-Baked Ham with Star Fruit Relish

2 large mangoes, peeled, pitted, cut into 1/2-inch pieces
4 star fruits, cut into 1/4-inch pieces
6 oranges (peeled and white pith removed), cut into 1/2-inch pieces
1 large red onion, finely chopped
1 large ripe tomato, cubed
1/4 cup fresh lime juice
1 tablespoon grated lime peel
Ground pepper to taste
Honey-baked ham

Combine first 7 ingredients in medium bowl. Season with generous amount of pepper. (May be prepared 2 hours ahead. Cover and refrigerate.) Serve with ham.

Yield: 10 servings.

Sunrise Shake

2 ripe bananas
4 ounces plain yogurt
2 papayas, peeled and seeded
2 tablespoons honey
1 cup low-fat milk
6 1/2 ounces chilled Perrier
Pinch of nutmeg

Place first five ingredients in blender. Blend on high speed until smooth. Stir in sparkling bottled water until frothy, and add nutmeg.

Yield: 2 servings.

Mango Muffins

Nothing could be nicer than the tropical taste of warm mango muffins for breakfast. And they are so quick and easy to make. Remember, overbeating results in a tough texture. Muffins baked in paper baking cups stay fresh longer. Leftovers can be frozen and reheated.

8 tablespoons unsalted butter, at room temperature
1/4 cup cornflake crumbs
3/4 cup packed light brown sugar
3 eggs
2 cups sifted all-purpose flour
1 tablespoon baking powder
1/2 teaspoon ground allspice
1 teaspoon salt
2 cups (about 2) ripe Brooks mangoes, peeled, pit removed, cut into 1/4-inch cubes
1 1/2 cups coarsely chopped walnuts or pecans
2 tablespoons dark rum
1 teaspoon grated lime zest

Preheat oven to 400 degrees. Lightly coat 24 muffin cups with 2 tablespoons of butter, or with nonstick cooking spray, or line them with paper baking cups. If not using paper liners, sprinkle with cornflake crumbs; tap out excess.

Stir and toss together the flour, baking powder, allspice and salt until completely mixed.

Place the remaining 6 tablespoons of butter in a large mixing bowl and beat either by hand or with electric mixer until light and fluffy. Gradually beat in brown sugar. Add eggs one at a time, beating well after each addition. Add the combined dry ingredients and beat just until the batter is blended; it should not be completely smooth. Fold in Brooks mangoes, walnuts, rum and lime zest. Spoon batter into prepared muffin cups, filling two-thirds full.

Bake for about 20 to 25 minutes or until tops are golden and a toothpick inserted in the center of a muffin comes out clean. Cool in pans on wire racks for 5 minutes before removing from pans.

Yield: about 2 dozen.

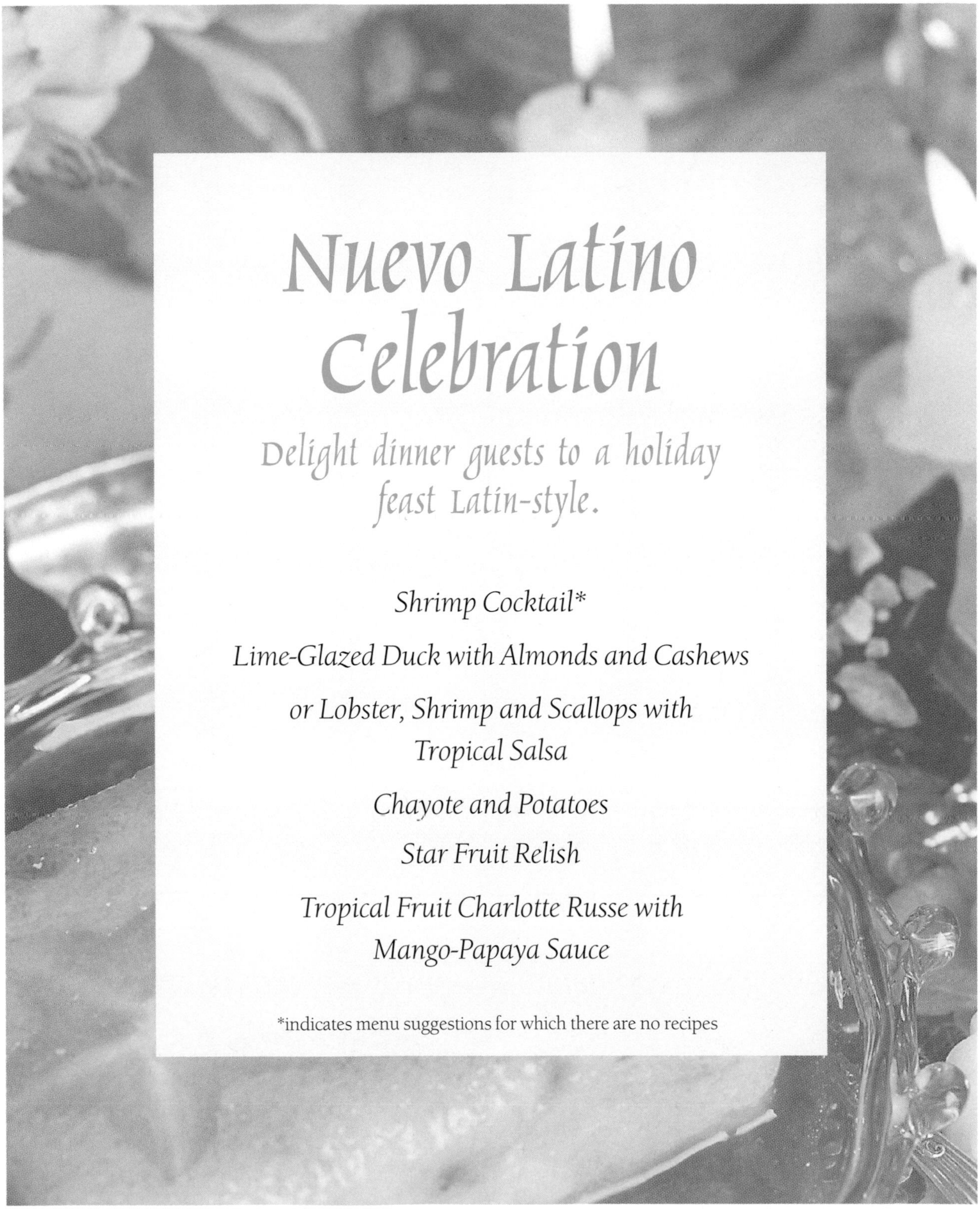

Nuevo Latino Celebration

Delight dinner guests to a holiday feast Latin-style.

Shrimp Cocktail*

Lime-Glazed Duck with Almonds and Cashews

or Lobster, Shrimp and Scallops with
Tropical Salsa

Chayote and Potatoes

Star Fruit Relish

Tropical Fruit Charlotte Russe with
Mango-Papaya Sauce

*indicates menu suggestions for which there are no recipes

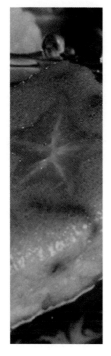

Lime-Glazed Duck with Almonds and Cashews

1 (4½- to 5-pound) duck
2 teaspoons salt
Pepper to taste
1 teaspoon sugar
2 teaspoons minced garlic
⅓ cup minced onion
2 teaspoons unsalted butter
½ cup apple jelly
½ teaspoon garlic
3 tablespoons spicy brown mustard
3 tablespoons heavy cream
¼ cup fresh lime juice
2 tablespoons finely chopped and seeded scotch bonnet pepper
    (wear rubber gloves)
¼ cup chopped almonds and cashews
2 teaspoons finely chopped fresh coriander

Preheat oven to 450 degrees. Prick duck all over and sprinkle with salt, pepper, sugar, and garlic. Arrange duck on a rack in a roasting pan and roast in middle of oven for 20 minutes. Reduce temperature to 350 degrees and loosely cover duck with foil. Roast duck for 1 hour more or until a meat thermometer inserted into thigh registers 160 degrees. Cool duck for 15 minutes and cut in half. Remove breast bones, being careful not to tear meat.

In a large skillet, cook onion in butter over moderately low heat, stirring until softened. Whisk in jelly until melted and add garlic, mustard, cream, a pinch of salt, lime juice and scotch bonnet. Bring glaze to a boil, stirring, and remove from heat.

Prepare grill. Brush duck halves with some glaze and grill over high heat, basting with remaining glaze, about 2 minutes on each side, until heated through. Arrange duck halves on platter and brush with any remaining glaze. Sprinkle duck with nuts and coriander.

Yield: 2 servings.

Lobster, Shrimp and Scallops with Tropical Salsa

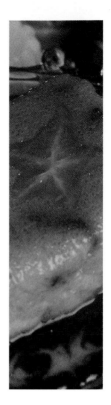

2 teaspoons vegetable oil
1 frozen lobster tail (about 3½ ounces), thawed, shelled, sliced
10 large uncooked shrimp, peeled, deveined
4 ounces sea scallops
1 (1-inch) piece fresh ginger, peeled, minced
1 small shallot, minced
1 large garlic clove, minced
1 tablespoon minced lime peel
1 teaspoon ground coriander
1 teaspoon lime juice
½ teaspoon curry powder
¼ teaspoon turmeric
⅛ teaspoon dried crushed red pepper
½ cup bottled clam juice
½ cup canned unsweetened coconut milk
Steamed rice
Tropical Salsa (page 51)

Heat 1 teaspoon oil in medium nonstick skillet over medium heat. Add lobster; sauté until almost cooked through, about 2 minutes. Transfer to bowl. Add shrimp and scallops to skillet; sauté until almost cooked through, about 2 minutes per side. Place seafood and pan drippings in bowl with lobster.

Heat 1 teaspoon oil in same skillet over medium-heat. Add ginger, shallot, garlic, lime peel, coriander, lime juice, curry powder, turmeric and crushed pepper; stir 1 minute. Add clam juice, coconut milk and juices from seafood; cook to sauce consistency, stirring occasionally, about 9 minutes. Add seafood; simmer until heated through, about 1 minute. Serve with steamed rice and Tropical Salsa.

Yield: 2 servings.

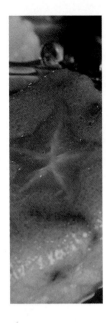

Chayote and Potatoes

1¼ pounds small boiling potatoes
Salt
¼ cup olive oil plus 2 teaspoons
1 tablespoon balsamic vinegar
⅛ to ¼ teaspoon white pepper
4 ounces lean bacon or prosciutto, cut crosswise into strips
6 ounces cremini mushrooms, quartered
2 garlic cloves, thinly sliced
1 pound chayotes, cut into strips
¼ cup fresh basil

Cover potatoes with cold water, add salt to taste and boil until tender 20 to 25 minutes. Combine ¼ cup olive oil and vinegar, 1 teaspoon salt and pepper in a separate bowl. Peel potatoes; quarter and toss with above dressing. Combine 1 teaspoon oil and bacon in a pan and cook until crisp. Discard excess fat. Add to potatoes and toss. Add 1 teaspoon oil, mushrooms, garlic, chayotes, and basil. Sauté for about 3 minutes. Drain and toss with potatoes. Salt and pepper to taste. Serve warm.

Yield: 4 servings.

Star Fruit Relish

2 yellow star fruit, sliced
1 medium-size sweet onion, sliced
1 large ripe pear, peeled and sliced
1 cup red wine vinegar
½ cup sweetened dried cranberries
¼ cup brown sugar
½ teaspoon ground cloves
½ teaspoon ground nutmeg
¼ teaspoon fresh lime juice
¼ teaspoon freshly ground black pepper
¼ teaspoon salt

Combine all of the ingredients in a large, nonreactive saucepan and cook over low heat, stirring occasionally. Simmer for 15 to minutes. Serve the relish immediately or refrigerate.

Yield: 2 cups.

Tropical Fruit Charlotte Russe with Mango-Papaya Sauce

Tropical fruits enliven this light and refreshing ending to a sophisticated menu.

1 Brooks mango
1 Brooks star fruit
$^1/_2$ Brooks Sunrise Solo papaya
1 cup strawberries, sliced
$1^1/_4$ cups orange juice
1 envelope gelatin
2 tablespoons Chambord Liqueur or orange liqueur

Cut the mango on either side of the pit. Scoop out the flesh; cut into $^1/_2$-inch cubes. Cut the star fruit into $^1/_2$-inch cubes. Cut the papaya in half, seed, peel, and cut into $^1/_2$-inch cubes. Place mango, starfruit, papaya, and strawberries in a 5x9-inch loaf pan. Place $^2/_3$ cup of orange juice in a small pan and sprinkle with the gelatin. Let soak for about 5 minutes. Heat very slowly until dissolved. Cool and add to remaining orange juice. Add the liqueur. Pour over the fruit in the loaf pan and chill for 4 hours or until set. Dip mold in hot water and invert onto a serving plate. Cut into slices and serve with Mango-Papaya Sauce.

Yield: 8 servings.

Mango-Papaya Sauce

1 Brooks mango
$^1/_2$ Sunrise Solo Papaya, peeled, seeded and sliced
$^1/_2$ cup orange juice

Cut the mango on both sides of the pit. Reserve a few slices for decoration. Scoop out all the rest of the flesh. Reserve a few papaya slices for decoration also. Place mango, papaya and orange juice in a blender or food processor fitted with the steel blade. Purée until smooth. Serve cold.

Glossary

Atemoya

The atemoya is a sweet and creamy delicacy, with an artichoke-like outer-skin and a smooth, rich pulp. This tropical fruit, grown in Florida, South America and the West Indies, makes for the perfect luxurious dessert presented in its most simple form: chilled, halved and served with a spoon!

History & Lore
The atemoya is part of a family of pudding-like fruits native to tropical America and the West Indies, and its introduction to the American palate is fairly recent. An employee of the United States Department of Agriculture "formulated" the atemoya in 1907, but mother nature had already seen to it that it was available in Australia in 1850 and again in Israel in 1930.

Selection, Care & Handling
Consumers should select pale green, relatively unblemished, hard or slightly soft fruit that has not been cracked open. Atemoyas often split slightly at the stem as they ripen, but it is best to purchase whole fruits at the market to avoid bacterial invasion. Once home, there is no real harm if the fruit opens—simply cover the ripening atemoya with a clean towel or napkin. Keep the fruit at room temperature and check often, because atemoya ripen very quickly; the fruit can then be refrigerated for several days.

Preparation/Serving Suggestions
The atemoya is ideally served in its natural form: chilled and halved, then scooped. Or, try quartering and seeding the atemoya and mixing it with other soft, mild fruits like papaya, mango and melon. For a simple, mellow sauce, purée the fruit and serve over sponge cake, poached fruit or pudding.

Nutritional Highlights
At 96 calories per $\frac{1}{3}$-cup serving, the atemoya is fairly high in calories, but is an excellent source of vitamins C and K, potassium and fiber.

Availability

Jan	Feb	Mar	Apr	May	Jun	Jul	Aug	Sep	Oct	Nov	Dec
							Aug	Sep	Oct	Nov	

Avocado

Florida's numerous avocado varieties differ in shape and size, but have in common green, smooth skin and comparatively low oil and high water contents. This variety is lower in fat, and not quite as rich tasting as the popular Hass variety grown in California and Mexico. Once considered an exotic product, avocado is quickly making its way into a wide variety of dishes in our culture, from salads to sandwiches to the ever-popular southwestern favorite, guacamole. But Brooks' light, tasty Florida avocado is enjoyed in a most simple form—right out of hand!

History & Lore
The avocado is native to Mexico, Central America and parts of South America and was cultivated by the ancient Mayas, Toltecs, Aztecs, Incas and other great Indian civilizations for centuries before the white man arrived in the New World. Early explorers were enthusiastic about the new-found fruit and took it back with them to Europe where it was gradually introduced throughout the areas with climates favorable to its culture. By 1825, avocado was growing in the Hawaiian Islands, Africa and Polynesia.

Selection, Care & Handling
Select fruit that yields gently to pressure and avoid avocados that look badly bruised or have dark, soft or sunken spots. To ripen hard avocados as quickly as possible, store them in a loosely closed paper bag at room temperature, checking the ripening process frequently. The fruit will not ripen when cut and a whole avocado should not be refrigerated, if possible.

Preparation/Serving Suggestions
Brooks' Florida avocado is a simple delicacy, served with just a touch of lime, salt and pepper. Avocado also adds a smooth, mellow flavor to sandwiches, salads, or guacamole, or cooked blended with eggs, fish or baked into soufflés and sauces.

Nutritional Highlights
A $\frac{1}{2}$-cup serving of avocado has about 96 calories and is an excellent source of potassium and vitamin A.

Availability

Jan	Feb	Mar	Apr	May	Jun	Jul	Aug	Sep	Oct	Nov	Dec
Jan	Feb	Mar			Jun	Jul	Aug	Sep	Oct	Nov	Dec

Boniato

This tropical sweet potato, also called dulce, resembles a cross between a Louisiana "yam" and an Idaho russet: semi-sweet and semi-dry, and very versatile. Sweetly aromatic, creamy-textured and much less sweet than our orange sweet potato, boniato is fluffier and feels slightly drier in the mouth. A boniato can be prepared successfully any way a common North American sweet potato is prepared.

History & Lore
Boniato is a true variety of the white or yellow fleshed sweet potato that originated in the tropics and subtropics and is quite different from the very sweet, orange-fleshed "sweet potato," or "yam," that Americans traditionally call by those names. The Cuban word boniato was first recorded in the Antilles in 1537 and was thought to have been used as an adjective to mean something sweet and harmless.

Selection, Care & Handling
Select rock hard tubers with no soft or moldy spots. The skin may be pinkish, purplish, cream, reddish and slightly patchy looking. Store boniato in a cool, dry, well-ventilated place at room temperature for no more than a few days.

Preparation/Serving Suggestions
Boniato can be prepared just as any sweet potato, but expect a nuttier, firmer, less sweet result that is easily overwhelmed with heavy seasoning, so go light on the additions. Boniato can be steamed, fried, boiled, sautéed, mashed and creamed into custards and flans, puddings, pies and muffins, and a baked boniato produces a very crusty and delicious skin. Peel boniatos under water to prevent discoloring, which occurs immediately after peeling; always keep covered in water while cooking, for the same reason.

Nutritional Highlights
Boniato has 115 calories per ½ cup serving and is extremely rich in vitamin A.

Availability

Jan	Feb	Mar	Apr	May	Jun	Jul	Aug	Sep	Oct	Nov	Dec

Calabaza

A versatile member of the squash family, calabaza is daily fare throughout Central and South America and the Caribbean and is growing in popularity in the United States. Also known as West Indian pumpkin, the calabaza has a bright orange flesh and green, tan or orange outer skin with mottled stripes and is relatively smooth and hard-shelled when mature. When cooked with other foods, or puréed, calabaza tastes best in stews, soups, gratins and other combination dishes.

History & Lore
The calabaza is native to the Americas and was a staple in the diets of Florida Indians and other early settlers, only recently beginning to reappear in North America. In Florida, the calabaza has been increasingly grown, and the vegetable is the chief ingredient in Caribbean and Latin American national favorite dishes.

Selection, Care & Handling
Consumers should pick calabaza that is relatively heavy for its size with a solid stem attached and a dull (not shiny) rind. The flesh should be closely grained and not dry or watery looking. Calabaza has a great shelf-life and stores whole superbly for a month in a well ventilated area. If the vegetable has been cut, cover it tightly with plastic and store in the refrigerator where it will remain fresh for about a week. Cooked, puréed calabaza will store well in the freezer for up to a year if packed in an airtight container.

Preparation/Serving Suggestions
Calabaza is utilized best when prepared with other foods—it generally does not fare well alone because it tends to turn out fibrous and watery. Calabaza is ideal for chunky or smooth soups, salads, purées, sauces, cakes, pies, custards, quick breads, cookies and puddings. Most recipes that call for pumpkin, butternut, acorn, buttercup or Hubbard squash will be equally tasty with calabaza. To prepare: use a heavy knife to cut off the stem, then cut the calabaza lengthwise and gently hammer the part of the blade that touches the squash to split it in two. Scoop out and discard the seeds and fibers and cut the vegetable into the appropriate size pieces, removing the rind with a paring knife.

Nutritional Highlights
At 35 calories per cup, calabaza is a great low-sodium choice for weight watchers and an excellent source of folic acid, potassium and vitamin A.

Availability

Jan	Feb	Mar	Apr	May	Jun	Jul	Aug	Sep	Oct	Nov	Dec

Chayote

This versatile vegetable, similar to squash, combines the taste and texture of zucchini and cucumber, and provides a delicate, sweet freshness to a variety of dishes. Usually apple-green to dark green in color, the chayote's skin is fairly smooth and its flesh is crisp and finely textured.

History & Lore

The chayote, grown on a thick vine, is most often found in the cuisines of the West Indies, South and Central America, India, North Africa, Indonesia, New Zealand and Australia. In many countries, the chayote's shoots, flowers and tuberous roots are eaten, and its nectar-rich blossoms are considered among the finest honey producers. The chayote is only grown in a few areas of the United States—Louisiana, Florida and the Southwest.

Selection, Care & Handling

Consumers should look for very firm, unblemished chayotes and store them lightly wrapped in the refrigerator. Unlike zucchini or other tender squashes, chayote can be stored for at least two weeks in the refrigerator, sometimes up to a month if in good condition.

Preparation/Serving Suggestions

Because the skin is fairly tough, chayote should be peeled, either before cooking with a vegetable peeler or afterwards by simply pulling off the skin. The flesh excretes a very slippery liquid that completely disappears in the cooking, and the large, edible seed should not be discarded—cooked along with the flesh, it tastes somewhere between a lima bean and an almond.

Prepared as a simple side dish, chayote can be either baked or sautéed, and its mellow flavor is often enhanced with garlic, shallot, onion or fresh herbs. Chayote also provides the base for a smooth, flavorful soup, a twist on traditional potato dishes or a delightful addition to a fresh, elegant salad. In Latin America, chayote is often served as dessert—stuffed with raisins, nuts, brown sugar and eggs!

Nutritional Highlights

Chayote is very low in calories—about 40 per cup, very low in sodium and a good source of potassium and fiber.

Availability

Jan	Feb	Mar	Apr	May	Jun	Jul	Aug	Sep	Oct	Nov	Dec

Coconut

An important and abundant fruit in all tropical cuisines, coconut is gaining popularity in the U.S. and has been enjoyed by our Latin American and Asian citizens for many years. Fresh coconut is a delicacy for its edible white flesh, clear liquid in the center of the nut and creamy milk obtained from squeezing the grated "meat."

History & Lore

The coconut is believed to have originated in southern Asia and the Malay Archipelago, and its buoyant and waterproof shell has enabled it to travel throughout the tropics, landing on small islands and low shores to become an extremely useful and versatile plant. In the tropical world, coconuts have been utilized fully: the wood of the tree to build houses and make furniture, the leaves to thatch dwellings and make fences, the oil extracted from the dry nut, the shell made into plates, bowls and spoons, and of course, the flesh, to be eaten.

Selection, Care & Handling

Fresh coconut sounds sloshy when shaken and has clean "eyes." The fruit should also be dry and free from mold or decay. Store whole coconut at room temperature; refrigerate chunks or freeze.

Preparation/Serving Suggestions

To prepare coconut, pierce the eyes and drain and chill the juice to drink or include in recipes. Tap the grooved shell with a hammer to crack it; then pry out the meat with a sturdy knife and peel if desired.

Nutritional Highlights

Coconut is fairly high in calories, at 139 per ½ cup, and fat at 14 grams, but is a good source of carbohydrates and potassium.

Availability

Jan	Feb	Mar	Apr	May	Jun	Jul	Aug	Sep	Oct	Nov	Dec

Ginger

Ginger is an aromatic addition and common flavoring that predominates in the Far East and is now sold fresh nationwide. Uniquely versatile, ginger adds zest to dishes and drinks, whether it is raw or cooked, sliced, grated, puréed, chopped or pressed to extract its juice.

History & Lore

Gingerroot is believed to be a native of tropical southeastern Asia and has been used for thousands of years. This golden-skinned root was carried from Asia into the Mediterranean and Europe and was later introduced into the West Indies and Mexico by the Spaniards. Today, ginger is a popular ingredient in Indian, Thai, Malaysian and Oriental cookery and is commercially produced in Hawaii, Puerto Rico, Fiji, Taiwan, Philippines, Costa Rica and Brazil.

Selection, Care & Handling

Select shiny, full, fresh-looking roots, avoiding any that are shriveled. Ginger can be stored for weeks if wrapped and refrigerated; cut off pieces as needed. Do not freeze, as this diminishes the fragrance.

Preparation/Serving Suggestions

Peel the skin, then grate, mince or slice the yellow flesh according to a recipe's requirements. To substitute fresh ginger for the ground spice, use about 1 tablespoon grated for $\frac{1}{4}$ teaspoon ground ginger. Ginger is ideal as a spicy addition to stir-fry recipes, marinades, flavoring for salad dressings, fruits, vegetables, seafood, poultry, meats and soups, and is also quite delicious steeped in hot water for teas and other beverages.

Nutritional Highlights

Because ginger is used in such small amounts, its nutrition and calorie counts are negligible. Five thin slices of ginger provide some vitamin C and potassium and contain 8 calories.

Availability

Jan	Feb	Mar	Apr	May	Jun	Jul	Aug	Sep	Oct	Nov	Dec

Guava

Guava is most easily recognized by its intense, tutti-frutti aroma and glorious pink flesh. Its flavor is most notably found in nectars, tropical punches and candies. The guava may be one of 140-odd species and the flesh may be sweet to sour, taste like strawberries, pineapple or banana and may be colored white to yellow to salmon to red.

History & Lore

Native to Brazil, the guava is also a hot commodity in Hawaii, Australia, India, Colombia, Venezuela, Mexico, South Africa and some parts of Southeast Asia, the Caribbean and a few groves in Florida and California. Unfortunately, guava is extremely susceptible to fruit-fly infestation so American consumers taste very few of the varieties available outside the U.S.

Selection, Care & Handling

Guava is typically hard to come by in produce sections, but consumers should look for the fruit from late spring to early fall. Shoppers should select yellow-green or pale yellow fruit, tender to the touch with a very rich, floral fragrance; as the fruit ripens, this aroma becomes increasingly distinct. If the fruit is slightly green, ripen it at room temperature, which will cause the yellow to become deeper and the skin softer. Keep close tabs on the ripening process of guava, as it can take anywhere from one to five days, and use it within two days after it reaches full ripeness.

Preparation/Serving Suggestions

Depending on the intended use, guava can be prepared in many different ways—out of hand, peeled, seeded and sliced, strained, puréed or poached. To eat fresh, cut-up guava, clip off the blossom end, halve the fruit lengthwise, scoop out the seedy pulp and cut the shell that remains. Guava is ideal for a luscious purée or as a base for custards, ices and mousses, rich sauces, guava paste, nectar or as a striking addition to a fruit mixture.

Nutritional Highlights

Each $\frac{1}{2}$-cup serving of guava has 45 calories and is low in sodium and high in potassium. Guava is also an extremely rich source of vitamin A and vitamin C.

Availability

Jan	Feb	Mar	Apr	May	Jun	Jul	Aug	Sep	Oct	Nov	Dec

Kumquat

A unique and intriguing fruit, kumquat has a small, oblong shape about one-and-a-half inches long, and looks like a miniature orange. The fruit serves as a tart treat to eat on its own, a beautiful garnish and a pungent addition to seafood, poultry, salads, stuffings, salsas, baked goods, ice creams, drinks and confections.

History & Lore
The kumquat was introduced into the United States in 1850 and has since been cultivated in small quantities in Florida and California. Brooks Tropicals sells the Nagami variety, with pungent sweet skin and a tart pulp. The fruit was actually considered a Citrus until 1915, when scientists found cellular differences sufficient to warrant moving it into its own genus, Fortunella.

Selection, Care & Handling
Kumquats are usually found in produce departments during the winter season and are often displayed loose, in baskets or plastic-filmed tray packs. The fruits should be firm like baby mandarins and stored at room temperature if being used within a few days of purchase. Otherwise, keep them refrigerated for up to about two weeks. Because of their thin skin, they tend to spoil more rapidly than oranges.

Preparation/Serving Suggestions
Kumquats are so unique because they can be served just as they appear whole—skin and all. If they are indeed to be served whole, simply rinse and dry the fruit; for most other preparations, the fruit will need to be seeded after slicing or halving lengthwise. As a garnish, thick slices of kumquats are perfect for cocktails and are a great substitute for orange-based dishes. Kumquats can also be blanched, sliced and seeded to add to stuffings, cakes and muffins or puréed to use in sauces, cakes, creams and frostings.

Nutritional Highlights
With a moderate amount of calories and a very low sodium count, kumquats are a good source of potassium and vitamin C.

Availability

Jan	Feb	Mar	Apr	May	Jun	Jul	Aug	Sep	Oct	Nov	Dec

Key Lime

Also called West Indian, bartender and Mexican lime, this small, thin-skinned yellowish fruit is prized for its bright aroma. Best known in Key lime pie, it is not, however, produced commercially in the Florida Keys. A brisk flavoring to use in the same way as lemon or the common Persian lime, Key limes will add more perfume.

Lime

Bright-green Florida Persian limes are the familiar market variety, relatively large in size, seedless and juicy. Limes enhance the flavor and visual appeal of drinks and dishes of almost any kind and are more fragrant and less acidic than lemons.

History & Lore
Like other citrus fruits, limes are believed to be native to southeastern Asia and have been cultivated for thousands of years. When Columbus made his second voyage to the Western Hemisphere in 1493 to establish a colony, he stopped at the Canary Islands and obtained seeds of various fruits and vegetables, including limes, to take with him. He planted the limes on the island of Hispaniola, in his settlement of Isabella. Later, Spanish conquistadores took limes from these groves with them to the mainland and planted them at St. Augustine, Florida.

Selection, Care & Handling
Select limes that look fresh, not leathery or shrivelled at the stem end. Avoid those with a brownish circle at the pointed end or any pitted areas, indicating rot or dryness. Refrigerate the fruit in a plastic bag up to a week.

Preparation/Serving Suggestions
Sweet, yet tart, limes are wonderful in refreshing drinks, exquisite desserts and flavorful salad dressings. To get the most juice from limes, keep at room temperature for one hour before squeezing; one medium lime contains approximately $1/4$ cup juice. Sprinkling lime juice on sliced apples, avocados, bananas and pears prevents discoloring, while serving a wedge of lime with papayas and other tropical fruits highlights their subtle flavors.

Nutritional Highlights
Limes are sodium-free, low in calories, high in vitamin C and a good source of fiber.

Availability

Jan	Feb	Mar	Apr	May	Jun	Jul	Aug	Sep	Oct	Nov	Dec

119
Glossary

Lychee

With a creamy white flesh reminiscent of a sweeter, more exotic grape, lychee is an exotic delicacy, revered as one of the most important Chinese fruits. The beautiful lychee tree features brilliant colored fruits that hang like bunches of strawberries, and the flesh is encased in a thin, crisp shell that is a rosy, brown color.

History & Lore

Lychee has been enjoyed in the Orient for over two thousand years and China remains the largest producer of the fruit. Smaller amounts are raised in Thailand, the Phillipines, Taiwan, India, South Africa, Australia, Hawaii, Mexico and Florida.

Selection, Care & Handling

Consumers should select the heaviest, fullest fruit with stems. The rosier the shell, the fresher the fruit, as mottling occurs shortly after picking. Avoid fruit light in weight, shriveled or cracked. A surprisingly durable fruit, lychee can remain fresh in the refrigerator for several weeks, although some of its perfumy aroma will be lost.

Preparation/Serving Suggestions

Lychee is truly enjoyed best straight, slipped fresh from the shell. Crack the shell lightly with a fingernail and slip out the translucent, gray-white pulp which has a large, mahogany-like seed. Lychees are also delicious peeled, halved and seeded to combine with other soft fruits like raspberries, kiwi, strawberries and mangoes.

Nutritional Highlights

Lychees are very low in calories and are an excellent source of vitamin C and potassium.

Availability

Jan	Feb	Mar	Apr	May	Jun	Jul	Aug	Sep	Oct	Nov	Dec

Malanga

A tropical staple, malanga is a starchy tuber with a texture and flavor similar to dried beans blended with waxy potatoes when boiled. Malanga is often used for chipping, as a creamy base for soups and stews and an interesting addition to spicy sausage and meat dishes. Also known as yautia and tannia, malanga is a versatile part of the daily diet in many cultures.

History & Lore

Malanga, which closely resembles another tropical staple, taro, has often been the subject of high confusion in the vegetable world. Malanga has some forty species, all native to the American tropics and including some of the oldest root crops in the world. This vegetable is actually the edible cormel (similar to a tuber) of a plant named Xanthosoma sagittifolium.

Selection, Care & Handling

Malanga should be light in color, very hard, with no shriveled or moldy patches. The skin is shaggy and brown and contains a beige, yellow or reddish flesh with a slippery, crisp texture. Pricking the skin with a fingernail will further help in choosing a fresh malanga: the flesh should be juicy and crisp, not soft or dry. Store the product at room temperature, no longer than a few days.

Preparation/Serving Suggestions

Malanga has a wide variety of uses, equally tasty as crispy chips, served with fish dishes and rich stews or as a unique base for a creamy soup. To prepare malanga, scrub the vegetable with a brush, trim off the ends and pare the skin. Rinse each piece and place in cold water to cover; the malanga can then be refrigerated for up to a day before cooking.

Nutritional Highlights

Malanga has 135 calories per ½ cup, cooked, and is a fairly good source of thiamine and riboflavin and contributes modest amounts of vitamin C and iron.

Availability

Jan	Feb	Mar	Apr	May	Jun	Jul	Aug	Sep	Oct	Nov	Dec

Mamey Sapote

On the outside, mamey sapote has a dull brown, football or softball shape, hiding a brilliant orangey-pink, sweet pulp that suggests sweet potato, avocado and honey. The flesh can be spooned directly out of its shell, diced for fruit cups, puréed with whipped cream or blended into a thick shake.

Selection, Care & Handling
Select fruit that is firm or slightly soft—mameys must be ripe before use. Leave at room temperature until it is avocado-tender all over. Refrigerate briefly if necessary. The mamey's leathery skin is easily peeled, much the same as an avocado. The fruit can then be sliced from the large, elliptical, shiny pit in the center.

Preparation/Serving Suggestions
Mamey sapote is a welcome addition to fruit compotes and poultry or fruit salads, puréed for a fruit shake, sauce for frozen desserts or used as a dip for crisp-textured fruits.

Nutritional Highlights
A 1/2-cup serving of mamey sapote contains about 100 calories and provides potassium and vitamins A and C.

Availability

Jan	Feb	Mar	Apr	May	Jun	Jul	Aug	Sep	Oct	Nov	Dec

Mango

The mango is more common than the apple in much of the world, where this tropical delight ranks second only to banana and coconut as a staple food. The aromatic, juicy flesh has been enjoyed more and more in the United States both in its natural form and as a delightful complement to a wide variety of dishes. Cultivated in as many shapes, sizes and colors as the apple, the mango is a tropical treat that has many ardent enthusiasts.

History & Lore
Mango is thought to have been cultivated for as long as 6,000 years and is a native fruit to Southeast Asia where more than three-quarters of the world's mangos are grown; India is the main producer. Mangos figured prominently in Hindu mythology and religious ceremonies; Buddha is said to have been presented with a mango grove as a place of repose. Plucked off the towering evergreen mango tree, this fruit is often enjoyed by poking a hole in its leather-like flesh and slurping the delicious nectar right from the source. In countries all over the world, mangos, whether eaten ripe, cooked or dried are a vital part of all meals.

Selection, Care & Handling
Select full, firm, partially ripe fruit that shows some hint of color, which ranges from green to orange to red and everything in between. Fresh mangos should always have some hint of scent. Consumers should sniff the stem end, detecting a pleasant scent of some sort, no matter how light. No perfume usually indicates the mango will have no flavor. If the smell is slightly alcoholic or sour, this means it has begun fermenting and should be rejected. Ripen a greenish mango at room temperature until tender to the touch and aromatic and chill briefly before serving, or up to a few days if the mango must keep.

Preparation/Serving Suggestions
Delicious in its natural form, peeled and sliced, the mango is also equally tantalizing in a variety of fruit and vegetable salads or for combined salads of chicken, pork or smoked meats. Mango makes for a wonderful purée, added to tropical drinks, parfaits, ice creams, mousses or frozen soufflés. To prepare a mango, vertically slice about 1/2 inch to the right of the stem so that it barely clears the long, flat narrow stone inside. Repeat on the other side, then cut the flesh from the seed. With a knife, either slice the halves and peel or score one side of the whole fruit into a gridlike pattern, peel the skin off and slice into halves.

Nutritional Highlights
Mango contains a rich abundance of vitamins A and C, is very low in sodium and high in potassium and fiber. A medium mango rakes in about 135 calories.

Availability

Jan	Feb	Mar	Apr	May	Jun	Jul	Aug	Sep	Oct	Nov	Dec

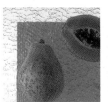

Papaya

Like its tropical companion, mango, the papaya is as common to natives south of the Tropic of Cancer as apples and oranges are to Americans. The Brooks papaya hails from the Caribbean and is pink-fleshed, yellow-skinned and pear-shaped with an aromatic pulp. This variety is unusually sweet and smooth, well suited to salads, fruit cups, shakes or cooked with meat or seafood. An extremely rich source of vitamins, the papaya is often considered one of nature's most perfect fruits.

History & Lore

The Spaniards discovered the papaya, or "tree melon" as it is often called, in tropical America during the sixteenth century, and the fruit was later introduced into the Philippines, Africa and Asia. The early Spanish settlers introduced papaya into Florida, and because of the tropical climate required for their growth, their production is largely limited to that state.

Selection, Care & Handling

The papaya is an extremely generous bearer, making the fruit available to us almost year-round. Select uniformly tender, mostly yellow or all-yellow fruit, and gauge a papaya's ripeness by touch, which should be similar to a ripe avocado. Spotting is usual and often indicates a more flavorful fruit. If the fruit is firm, soften at room temperature in a dark place; this process can be accelerated by placing the papaya in a paper bag with a banana, which produces ethylene, a natural gas that speeds up the ripening process. When ripe, a papaya will emit a soft, fruity aroma.

Preparation/Serving Suggestions

Papaya's subtle, sweet flavor is a welcome addition to fruits like pineapple, strawberry, orange, banana, coconut or lime and a new twist on old favorites like upside-down cakes, fresh fruit tarts and puddings. In its puréed form, papaya makes a unique dressing, daquiri or base for ice creams and sherbets, and its edible seeds are an interesting addition sprinkled on salads. The fruit also perfectly complements marinated meats, roasts or fish, as it never becomes mushy when cooked. Papaya is simple to prepare, needing only to be halved and seeded, as you would a cantaloupe. The thin skin is easily removed with a vegetable peeler.

Nutritional Highlights

Papaya is an extremely rich source of vitamin C and is high in potassium and fiber. A cup of papaya contains 55 calories. The milky juice of a papaya contains an enzyme called papain—a common ingredient in meat tenderizers and highly regarded as a remedy for indigestion.

Availability

Jan	Feb	Mar	Apr	May	Jun	Jul	Aug	Sep	Oct	Nov	Dec

Passion Fruit

A truly unique and sensual fruit, the passion fruit has an intense, aromatic flavor, reminiscent of jasmine, honey and citrus. Natives of tropical and subtropical climates, where the fruit thrives, feast on the passion fruit's exquisite juices in large numbers. With Florida crops filled out by those in California and New Zealand, passion fruit is available year round and is beginning to enjoy a larger following among North Americans.

History & Lore

Enjoyed in tropical and subtropical paradises around the world, including New Zealand, South America, Kenya and Hawaii, the passion fruit evokes much pleasure among its consumers, as its name suggests. But passion fruit's namesake is actually a reference to the Passion of Christ. The different parts of this fruit's beautiful flower represent the wounds, crucifixion nails, crown of thorns and the Apostles.

Selection, Care & Handling

Select full and heavy red, yellow, lavender or dark purple fruit, which is ready to eat when it is creased and sounds sloshy when shaken. Keep smooth, rounded unripe fruit at room temperature for a few days until creased. Once ripe, passion fruit will store in the refrigerator for about a week, or in the freezer for months if stored in plastic bags. When ready to use, simply halve the fruit and scoop out the pulp.

Preparation/Serving Suggestions

Passion fruit works best as a flavoring, used similarly to vanilla or Cognac, because it has such an intense, perfumy flavor. With its tart, citrus, honey and floral flavor, the fruit perfectly suits seafood and poultry, salad, drinks, desserts and fruit mixtures, or is equally good spooned over cakes, sherbet, yogurt or ice cream.

Nutritional Highlights

Passion fruit is low in sodium, with relatively good amounts of vitamins A and C and high amounts of fiber.

Availability

Jan	Feb	Mar	Apr	May	Jun	Jul	Aug	Sep	Oct	Nov	Dec

Scotch Bonnet Pepper

The Scotch Bonnet Pepper, also known as the Habanero chili-pepper, ranges in heat from mild to incendiary. This flavorful pepper, whether green, yellow, orange or red, adds a memorable taste and kick when handled judiciously.

Since the Scotch Bonnet Pepper is very thin-skinned, it is quite perishable and will only last a few days, wrapped in plastic in the refrigerator.

Availability

Jan	Feb	Mar	Apr	May	Jun	Jul	Aug	Sep	Oct	Nov	Dec

Star Fruit

With its unique and tantalizing appearance and light, juicy taste, the star fruit is quickly making its mark as a consumer and foodservice staple—the perfect accompaniment to a fruit melange or an eye-pleasing garnish to almost any sophisticated dinner entrée. While the star fruit is indeed an interesting fruit to look at in its whole form, its true charm appears when it has been sliced crosswise, forming a perfect star. Whatever the venue, the star fruit, also called carambola, is a tropical treasure to behold.

History & Lore

The star fruit is a vital crop in Asia, South and Central America, the Caribbean and Hawaii. The fruit is thought to have been a native of the Malayan archipelago that eventually made its way to China. From there, it is believed that Chinese immigrants to Hawaii, or perhaps sandalwood traders on route to the West, brought this luscious fruit to the attention of the New World.

Selection, Care & Handling

Choose firm, partly or fully yellow fruit, avoiding those with browned, shriveled ribs, and allow to ripen at room temperature until the fruit is completely golden. When star fruit is at its peak eating time, the fruit will have a full floral-fruity aroma—this indicates that it is at full development. The most tart star fruit has very narrow ribs, while the sweet yellow varieties have thick, fleshier ribs. The fruit will store in the refrigerator for about two weeks, depending upon their condition when purchased.

Preparation/Serving Suggestions

A refreshingly easy fruit to prepare, the star fruit is best enjoyed when simply rinsed and thinly sliced, allowing its unique blend of apples, grapes and citrus to be fully savored by the consumer. If the ribs are browned and unsightly, simply use a vegetable peeler to shave off the darker stripe of skin. Star fruit works well as a trendy alternative to the traditional garnishes, especially if the fruit is on the sour side. Lightly sautéed, they beautifully complement poultry, seafood and meat and are ideal for fruit cups. The sweeter varieties can be used more predominantly in fruit salads and other fresh desserts.

Nutritional Highlights

A medium star fruit is very low in calories (40) and is an excellent source of vitamin C, potassium and fiber.

Availability

Jan	Feb	Mar	Apr	May	Jun	Jul	Aug	Sep	Oct	Nov	Dec

Sugar Cane

Sturdy canes of bamboo-like sugar are a familiar sight in the tropics. Peeled pieces of stalk are chewed to release the thin, flavorful, sweet juice—satisfying and rewarding, especially for children. The canes, peeled and split lengthwise, are also used as tasty skewers to grill seasoned ground meat mixtures, particularly in Southeast Asian dishes.

Availability

Jan	Feb	Mar	Apr	May	Jun	Jul	Aug	Sep	Oct	Nov	Dec

123
Glossary

Taro

A tropical staple food, taro, also known as dasheen, is a starchy, substantive food when cooked, with a flavor of a cross between chestnut and artichoke hearts. This dense, versatile tuber is delicious as crunchy chips and fritters, in soufflé, hearty stew or as a wonderfully thick and creamy base for soup.

History & Lore

As the main ingredient for the revered, Hawaiian dish, poi, taro has been used on these islands for years to make large quantities of this unusual paste. The vegetable probably originated in the East Indies and is a popular item throughout the Pacific Islands, much of the Orient, the Caribbean, North Africa and small areas of South and Central America.

Selection, Care & Handling

Taro is brown, hairy and barrel-shaped, with distinct rings and a very white, or lilac-gray flesh, sometimes speckled with tiny brown flecks. A particularly small form of taro, called eddo, is a Brooks standard and is favored by the Chinese, Japanese and in the Caribbean. Select dry, very hard tubers without any mold or shriveling. The cut flesh should smell fresh and look juicy. Store taro in a cool, well ventilated place—not the refrigerator—for no more than a few days. Use the tuber as soon as it becomes the slightest bit soft.

Preparation/Serving Suggestions

Once cooked, taro turns color from very bright white to cream, gray or purplish and is best served boiled or steamed to serve with stews. Taro should be served very hot, as it becomes dense and waxy once cool and has a tendency to dry out so should be doused with butter or meat juices. Taro can be cooked, then puréed for additions to fritters and soufflés and is wonderful deep-fried in thin chips or grated into pancakes. To prepare taro, slice off the ends, pare deeply to remove all skin and discolored spots, then place in cold water at once. The acrid juice contained in taro may be irritating, so oil your hands or wear gloves if bothersome.

Nutritional Highlights

Taro is an excellent source of potassium and a good source of iron and fiber. One-half cup contains about 100 calories.

Availability

Jan	Feb	Mar	Apr	May	Jun	Jul	Aug	Sep	Oct	Nov	Dec

Uniq Fruit

Uniq fruit, often marketed by the trademark name, ugli fruit, suggests a flavor somewhere between a mandarin and a grapefruit. Similar in its ranges of uses to other members of the citrus family, uniq fruit is especially delightful peeled and sectioned right out of hand—a refreshing treat and wonderful change of pace from the ordinary orange.

A Uniq History

The uniq fruit was discovered as an accidental seedling in Jamaica where it was propagated and exported beginning in the 1930s. Uniq fruit is now available from Brooks Tropicals.

Preparation/Serving Suggestions

Uniq fruit ranges in size from a large navel orange to that of a hefty grapefruit. Its puffy, thick skin makes the uniq fruit much easier to peel than other citrus fruits and usually ranges in color from lime-green to a light orange. The fruit's yellow-orange flesh is relatively free of seeds and is very juicy once cut. Uniq fruit can be enjoyed in much the same way as other citrus fruits and is especially wonderful eaten peeled and sectioned. The fruit may be halved like a grapefruit or used as a light addition to fruit or vegetable salads, gelatin desserts, and compotes. Peel and segment uniq fruit as you would other citrus.

Selection, Care & Handling

Look for uniq fruit that is heavy for its size, with no sign of drying at the stem end. The fruit often has some natural traces of mottling, bronzing, surface scarring, or uneven coloring. Because of uniq fruit's thick skin it may be stored for up to 2 weeks in a commercial cooler at 50 to 55 degrees.

Nutritional Highlights

Uniq fruit is a good source of vitamin C and is high in fiber.

Availability

Jan	Feb	Mar	Apr	May	Jun	Jul	Aug	Sep	Oct	Nov	Dec

Water Coconut

The juice of immature coconut in its green husk is a favorite refresher in the tropical heat. The top of the coconut is hacked off like a soft-boiled egg, and the clear, cool sweet drink sipped through a straw. The delicate, gelatinous flesh is spooned up and savored, for an added treat.

Availability

Jan	Feb	Mar	Apr	May	Jun	Jul	Aug	Sep	Oct	Nov	Dec

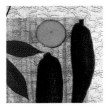

Yuca

In Hispanic culture, this tuberous vegetable, highly starchy and chewy in texture, is served in some form throughout the meal, used in stews, flatbreads, dumplings and puddings. Yuca, also commonly known as casava, is most familiar in its common form as tapioca. Boiled, it is soft and very sticky, with a buttery flavor, while fried it is sweet and crunchy, a particularly favorite form of eating yuca in the Caribbean.

History & Lore

Yuca is native to Brazil and is now cultivated throughout South and Central America, the Caribbean, Africa, Asia, the South Pacific and Florida, with various cultures adapting it to suit their tastes. In East Africa, yuca is often served with beef in a rich sauce of onion, tomato, coconut milk and spices, while in South America it is used as potatoes are used in many of our stews, and in Nigeria it is often cooked with salt herring.

Selection, Care & Handling

Choose hard tubers without mold, cracks or slime and make sure the flesh is as bark-covered as possible. Yuca should smell clean and fresh, with a clear, coconut-white interior and no darkening or grayish-blue fibers should appear near the skin. Yuca spoils very rapidly, so you will need to use it soon after purchase. If you truly need to store it, keep yuca uncovered in a cool place other than the refrigerator and slice off what is needed, allowing the yuca to naturally seal up its cut surface. Peeling, covering and immersing in water is an option, but the vegetable tends to lose most of its flavor this way.

Preparation/Serving Suggestions

Yuca is fairly bland, so it is ideally suited to salty, spicy and hot sauces and its gummy texture is compatible to boiling, frying, sautéing and for use in stews. Grated, yuca can be incorporated into cakes, breads and puddings. To prepare yuca, scrub each tuber, hack into convenient lengths, then slit the bark and with a knife, pull it off along with the pink underlayer. Rinse well, then place in cold water.

Nutritional Highlights

Yuca is high in calories, about 135 per $\frac{1}{2}$ cup and is a good source of iron and calcium.

Availability

Jan	Feb	Mar	Apr	May	Jun	Jul	Aug	Sep	Oct	Nov	Dec

125
Glossary

Index

127
Index

Additional copies of *Floribbean Flavors*
may be obtained from Brooks Tropicals, Inc.
1-800-327-4833